30
Day
Blackout

By Stacy Jagger

with Elizabeth Adams

First Edition September 2019

Cover Design by Caitlin Daschner at Chromantic Studio
Illustrations by Cheyenne Cox

Published by Stacy Jagger
www.StacyJagger.com

For my grandmother, Florence.
Thanks for teaching me what safe felt like.

Contents

"PLAY IS OFTEN TALKED ABOUT AS IF IT WERE A RELIEF FROM SERIOUS LEARNING. BUT FOR CHILDREN, PLAY IS SERIOUS LEARNING. PLAY IS REALLY THE WORK OF CHILDHOOD."

— FRED ROGERS

Foreword

By William Sears, M.D.

This must-read, and must-do, book is written from the heart of a mother and the long experience of a family therapist. As I have been saying for decades, parenting, in a nutshell, is giving your children the tools to succeed in life. Think: empathy, compassion, engagement, love of nature, and the greatest of Mom's formulas for raising happy, healthy kids, "Go outside and play." Excessive screen time sabotages Mom's wisdom.

During a recent holiday family dinner, I put a sign on the entry door to our home: "Welcome to The Fun House! Please deposit cellphones here," with a big arrow pointing down to the deposit basket. Of course, I got a few looks of, "Oh, Grandpa…" and a few raised eyebrows from the cellphone-attached adults. It's interesting that the adults seemed to have had more of a problem with my wish than did their children.

I noticed that, after a few minutes of imagined boredom (mother of eight, Martha, always told our children: "Boredom is a choice…"), the kids were really getting into the fun and games. They were enjoying camaraderie instead of cellphones; dinner-table talk instead of screen-checking. That day they got out of themselves and enjoyed others.

The eye-to-eye contact that parents encourage in bringing up successful children is being downgraded in favor of eye-to-screen contact. And, as Stacy Jagger so eloquently states: "Screens are coming between us."

This book is a riveting read. I guarantee that no matter what your cellphone-use bias is, by the time you finish this book you will be motivated to believe that most families suffer from what we in our pediatric office call CPA – cellphone addiction.

Children walk into my office holding their cellphones and as I'm about to start an examination a wise parent will often admonish their child about CPA. "Please put away your cellphone and pay attention to Dr. Bill..." I restrain myself from asking, "Why didn't you leave your child's cellphone in the car?" Well, now that I have read Stacy's book, I will go ahead and say it!

The overuse of screen time reminds me very much of how we pediatricians have struggled to convince parents that junk food creates junk behavior and junk learning. Our simplistic advice, "Feed your child better food..." and so on wasn't getting results. It took shock statements like, "Your daughter is prediabetic..." and "Your son is pre-Alzheimer's..." to get the parents' attention. Finally sweetened-beverage consumption is going down; yet are screens replacing sweets, and having a similar brain-dumbing and even addicting effect?

Now's the time for parents, teachers, and all persons who have the best interests of children in mind to take action on the smart use of screen time or, as we pediatricians call it, "The largest experiment on childhood brain development in the history of mankind." Yes, you read that right. The beautiful brains of growing children are being seriously compromised by CPA. Already the incidence of ADHD is increasing yearly, now between five and ten percent of school children, so do we really need another dose of *hyperarousal* in already overstimulated children? Do we really want our children to carry around a pocket device that causes disruptive dings all day long? Get ready to learn a term that I use to summarize the concerns that we pediatricians have about the effects of screen time overuse and abuse on children's developing minds. *Glucocorticoid neurotoxicity.* Sounds like something you don't want your children to have. It describes the damaging effects of prolonged high levels of stress hormones on the vulnerable and rapidly developing pre-teen and teen brain.

12

Before giving you a glimpse of what science says about the smart use of screen time, let me interject a ray of light into smart cellphone use. In our upcoming book, *The Healthy Brain Book*, I have a section entitled "The Grateful Brain" where we show it's important that persons of all ages practice daily exercises in the attitude of gratitude. Cellphones help this happen. I encourage my patients, and our grandchildren, to keep a list of "gratitudes" – special events and special people in their lives that make them smile and feel grateful for the life they are living. Then when they go through a downer or feel that their life "sucks," they can easily open their cellphone notepad and review some of what they have learned to be grateful for. This is a quick way to get them out of their funk and helps parents interject a bit of positivity in modern technology.

Another thing I like about *30 Day Blackout* is that Stacy supports her advice with solid science, drawing on what experts around the world advise about smart cellphone use. Here is an example of this research:

There's a dose-dependent association between metabolic syndrome (pre-diabetes and obesity) and screen time in adolescents. The term "dose dependent" means, in simple yet scary terms, the more time you spend in front of a screen the more excess fat you accumulate throughout your body. What's interesting about this study is it also occurred in teen athletes, showing that increased exercise does not cancel out excess screen time as a health risk.

In this book the author highlights a behavior that is infecting the lives of older teens and young adults: Social anxiety. To get along, they go along with the cellphone crowd. As a result, they are becoming more comfortable relating to screens and more uncomfortable relating eye-to-eye, face-to-face with real people. In my pediatric practice, I see a behavior that affects a teen's physical appearance: a humped-over posture resulting

13

from "text neck" that needs to be corrected. This humped-over posture itself would interfere with social interaction.

Stacy takes you through each step on the path to surviving and thriving during the 30 Day Blackout with your family. As you follow her real-life success stories of families who have done this, one consistent perk emerges: All family members become better connected to each other instead of their screens.

I highly recommend this book. Read it, do it, and then watch your family transform from "sit and watch" to "move and play".

William Sears, M.D.
Co-Author of *The Dr. Sears T5 Wellness Plan*:
Makeover Your Mind and Body, 5 Changes in 5 Weeks

Introduction

I'll never forget the Thompson family that came to see me years ago. Five children—all in the hallway outside my office—fighting, yelling, name calling, slapping each other. It was like a bad episode of *The Three Stooges*, except there were more of them, all young children, and the mother was about to pull her hair out.

From a well-to-do family, these children had successfully fired all their caregivers— every nanny they had ever had, quit. The parents had been working on their fast-growing company and had relinquished care of their children to nannies and screens for years. Mrs. Thompson knew her family life had reached critical mass, and the problem wasn't getting any better. She was desperate for help. It was not only affecting their home life, but there were plenty of academic and social concerns for her children, as well. Not to mention there wasn't a nanny in town that would take that position. Family therapy was their final hope.

Honestly, as I looked at this family swimming in dysfunction, I knew there was no way I could help them unless major changes were made. When I asked during my intake how much screen time the children had each day, I got a blank, confused stare, which I eventually realized meant ALL DAY. They watched multiple screens, with almost no breaks unless someone was snoring.

I am an expressive arts and play therapist, which means I have a way of working with children using their own language—the language of creativity and play. My office is full of art materials, musical instruments, puppets, sand trays, a dollhouse. You get the picture. Children who are in a high state of arousal from too much entertainment-based screen time come into my office thinking that I must be there to entertain them, too.

Well, I'm not. Believe it or not, everything in my office serves a purpose for facilitating a therapeutic experience.

Without the removal of screens for a time, I knew there was no practical way I could give this family what they needed. Suddenly, I was inspired. I imagined them going on a fast. Not a fast from food, but a fast from screens. I called it, "The 30 Day Turn It Off Challenge." My private practice was new and my experience dealing with these specific issues was relatively limited. But I knew these children needed drastic changes immediately.

I somehow convinced the parents of our plan of action. Their willingness was a clear indicator of their desperation. At the time, I knew very little about the science of the negative effects of screen time on the nervous system, but I knew what I had practically observed. I knew how I handled screens with my own children, but back then, I didn't have years of experience with hundreds of families to draw on like I do now.

What I *did* have were memories of a time years ago when my husband Ron and I were newly married, and we went to visit a friend's farm that was about an hour outside Nashville. On their 150 acres sat a cabin from the 1850s, completely devoid of all modern conveniences. There was no electricity, no running water, no indoor plumbing. It had three rooms plus a loft, and we adventurously decided we wanted to spend a weekend there to experience life "unplugged."

Now, understand we were young and had no children, and I was a frustrated adventurer who wanted to get away from my hometown. One of those nights as we were about to go to sleep, I turned to my husband and said, "I want to live here." He looked at me like I was nuts.

"I want to live here, just for a few months, and experience life unplugged from everything."

I didn't understand at the time why living in the middle of the woods without electricity seemed so appealing to me. I was just young enough and crazy enough to try something completely off the wall. This trait, though severely toned-down, has thankfully followed me into middle age.

My upbringing was haphazard at best. My family was evicted from nearly every home I ever lived in. There was constant fighting, incessant chaos, my father's drinking, my mother's nervous breakdowns, the constant barrage of television, and my failed attempts to feel better by engaging in unhealthy relationships. My body and spirit were exhausted. Somehow, I knew that I needed a rest—a reset.

The complete calm and quiet were calling me. I felt like Jenny from *Forrest Gump*, who just needed to sleep a while after indulging in her partying lifestyle—except I didn't have a safe place to rest. I seemed to find myself spinning all the time on the inside, and I couldn't jump off the crazy train.

I needed a do-over. A reset. A calm place to just "be."

So, being the supportive, understanding, if-that's-what-you-need-let's-do-it husband he is, Ron was willing to try it. About a week later, he called our friends who owned the cabin, not quite sure how to ask such an off-the-wall question.

But when our friend answered the phone, she immediately said, "Ron, I was thinking about you and Stacy just this morning when I was walking the dogs out by the cabin. I was remembering how much fun you guys had out here. I wish the two of you could come out here for a few months and live!"

Suspecting she was joking but hoping she wasn't, Ron replied, "Well, it's funny you would mention that."

It was fate.

I was a ballroom dance instructor at the time, and my hair dryer, curling iron, and makeup were prime necessities given my job. So, it was bordering on miraculous, or certifiably insane, that I actually wanted to do this. I cannot really explain to you how I knew it was the right thing to do, but it's a feeling I call God's Delight, which usually feels like a mix of faith and crazy. We knew we needed an adventure. Well, at least *I* knew, and my husband was willing to orchestrate it.

We packed up every electronic item we owned, put it all into storage, and headed to the woods for what we expected to be a three-month hiatus from modern conveniences. My mom agreed to let me stay with her when I was desperate for a hot bath, and if I had a formal event to attend, I could get ready at a friend's house.

We packed a cooler with ice and lunch meat, bought some kerosene lamps, and made our way to the farm. We had virtually no other plan but to get out there and figure it out.

As our third month was drawing to a close, we spent the weekend at Opryland Hotel following a ballroom event. We lounged around, enjoying the convenience of lights and hot water and hair dryers. Of all things, we watched a marathon of the reality show, "The Pioneer Life," which hit a climactic point when they neared their first winter. And that gave me another crazy idea.

"Do you think we could make it in that cabin through the winter?"

"I don't know," replied Ron, but I could tell his engineer's mind was already sorting out the logistics.

We decided to give it a shot. We made it to spring somehow, and then through another summer and fall. In the end, we stayed in that non-electric cabin for 18 months.

In case you're wondering why I'm telling you all of this, you need to know that I wouldn't take a million dollars for the lessons I learned living in that cabin. I learned the power of slow. I learned how to go for a three-mile walk with our sheepdog Max, and how to come home to the cabin and take a long nap with no clocks ticking, no refrigerator humming, nothing but the sounds of nature all around me. I learned how to listen to the wind. I learned how to sit and watch the trees, how to keep a garden, how to spend hours chatting with a neighbor. I hiked every morning and showered in a barn in a converted horse trough. I learned to enjoy those walks in the wide, open spaces.

What I didn't know then, but I know now, is that I was allowing my nervous system to regulate for the first time in my life. I was imprinting a new pattern of mindfulness into my lifestyle that would allow my brain to notice what I was seeing, hearing, smelling, tasting, touching—in the present moment. I was fully grounded for the first time, ever.

I was raised in such chaos that my brain perceived almost everything as a threat, as unsafe, and my nerves were literally shot, meaning my sympathetic nervous system was in a constant state of fight, flight, or freeze, which can be a torturous way to live. As anyone with trauma history knows, this is our everyday reality. Unplugging for a time was the kindest gift I could have given myself, even though my friends and family thought I had lost my mind. Some still do.

That whole experience was on my mind as I spoke with the Thompson family. Having experienced my own extreme Blackout, I intuitively knew what this family needed. Given the fact that no one even knew how much screen time the children were actually watching, much less the content, they needed an intervention. The father, embarrassed by his children's behavior, and the mother, at her own wit's end, were ready to do just about anything I recommended, no matter what it took.

19

This was the only family in my years of recommending the Blackout who repeated it six times. Yes, you read that right. Six times!

During the first 30 days, the children were basically holding their breath until it was over—counting down the days until they could have their precious devices back in their hands. The father was absolutely committed to the process, and the mother was hanging on for dear life, hoping a change was on the horizon.

They had their family meeting in my office—the father sat down with his children to explain to them that until he saw kindness and respect in their family, he would not be returning any devices, and that he was truly sorry for allowing their family to get to this point. There was not a babysitter in town that would even attempt to help take care of them, he had to work, and their mother was exhausted. Basically, he just wasn't having it anymore. So, they did it again. And again. And again... to the tune of six months!

To this day, if those children see me in town, they turn and run the other direction.

But the father got his point across, the children had a re-parenting experience (as did the parents), and they gained much needed wisdom and insight in the process of helping their children find more productive things to do with their time than stare at a screen. And, not only did they get their time back, they got their kids back—plus their sanity, serenity, and peace of mind.

These experiences are why I recommend a 30 Day Blackout to families, and how I know full well that it will not kill them. Taking a much-needed rest from the constant barrage of notifications and screens and games will be a positive experience—eventually.

The Blackout may sound crazy to you, or to your partner, or to your family and friends. But have faith.

And hey, at least you're not moving to a non-electric cabin.

How This Book Works

This book is a roadmap of the 30 Day Blackout, a hiker's guide, if you will. It's almost always the first step in a program I designed called The Mountain Method. Think of the Blackout as hiking to base camp.

In my practice, I work closely with parents to determine where the family is now and where they would like to be. Some want to transition through a divorce smoothly. Others have children who are cutting and suicidal. Some are being bullied at school or struggling with compulsive behaviors they can't control.

The smooth transition, the healing of pain and trauma, the coping mechanisms and cessation of unwanted behavior are the families' goals at the summit, the top of the metaphorical mountain I am helping them to climb. But before you strap on your climbing gear, you must hike to base camp. This book is how you get there. It does not cover the entire Mountain Method, but it is a detailed guide to the Blackout.

You'll see interviews from other parents who implemented the Blackout and what it looked like for them. You'll hear stories of clients in my office, from mild to extreme cases, though their names and situations will be modified to protect their privacy. I'll explain the science behind the technique and some of the methods I use in family therapy.

I'll walk you through the steps of the Blackout, explain why you should or should not do certain things, and tell you what to expect. At the end of each chapter there are questions I strongly suggest you answer. They will help you get the most out of this process. I recommend reading the whole book (or at least through

Chapter 5), before beginning the Blackout, then referring back to specific chapters and answering the questions as you go through the process. Highlighting passages you think might pertain to your family will make it easier to reference them as you go along.

I will often speak directly to you, the reader, in a sort of simulation of family therapy. This is both to help you understand the process as you would if you were my client, and also because many people do not have access to a family therapist, due to location, finances, schedule, or a host of other reasons.

This book is not just for parents, but for anyone responsible for children—teachers, grandparents, caregivers. I will use the word "partner" to refer to whomever you are co-parenting with. This may be your spouse, your ex-spouse, a boyfriend or girlfriend, a parent, grandparent, sibling, or friend. Families come in all shapes and sizes. Your partner is whoever is in the trenches with you; the person who has your back, or who at least loves your child as much as you do.

At the end of the book are resources you can use to facilitate your Blackout and your general family health. You'll find links to more information, book recommendations, materials and suggestions, and support groups. If you feel you could benefit from a family therapist, there are links for that as well.

This book is not intended to replace face-to-face therapy or medical care. It cannot diagnose you or your child. Please seek help from your doctor or psychiatrist/therapist if you need it. We all need a little help sometimes and it's okay to ask for it.

Best of luck to you on the hike. I'm cheering you on.

Stacy

1

Hijacked

Caroline was ten years old and suicidal. Pulling her hair out by the handful. She was depressed, lost, and unreachable.

Matthew was shut down, emotionally absent, and unable to connect with his own family. He didn't participate in games; he didn't have an opinion.

Charlotte was six years old and suddenly began wetting her pants. At school, at home, while running errands. Her parents had recently divorced, and her world had turned upside down.

Sadly, these cases are not as uncommon as you might think. We tend to hide our children's most damaging behavior from those around us, like a shameful secret. We don't tell our friends for fear of looking like a bad mom or a clueless dad. We don't want to admit that things have gotten completely out of control or that we don't know what to do.

Maybe you recognize your child in some of these cases. Maybe you see your nephew or niece. Your grandchild. Your student. The kids you take care of.

You probably know kids like David and Ethan. They were out of control. Distracted, hyper, unmanageable. Tantrums abounded, fights were frequent, and nothing their parents tried helped.

And then there's Maya. One day, Maya started stealing. Small things at first, then bigger and bigger, from riskier and riskier locations. She had everything she needed and most of what she wanted, yet she couldn't resist the urge to slip that trinket into her pocket.

Maybe you know a child like Maddy. Maddy quit speaking entirely. No words, only grunts when she wanted something. She never made eye contact. She never hugged her parents back or joined her siblings for a game. She would only play video games alone in her room.

Each of these children was a patient in my office. Each of them was a victim of screens, of unregulated technology and disconnected families. I guided each of their families through the 30 Day Blackout. I watched these children heal, return to themselves, and discover their own creativity. You'll see their full stories throughout the book.

In my years as a Licensed Marriage and Family Therapist and a counselor to children, I have seen hundreds of families suffering from a number of issues: divorce, loss of a parent or child, bullying, sexual abuse, pornography, substance abuse. The list goes on. In many of these cases, the families have lost the ability to connect with each other, and they feel isolated—spouse to spouse, parents to children, children to their siblings. And I see one overarching, primary cause of this alienation within families.

If you are reading this book, I suspect you know where I'm going. Screens have hijacked our time and our personal lives. They demand our attention and steal it away from where it rightfully belongs. We feel busier than ever, yet we're not getting half as much done as we'd like to. **We feel disconnected from our lives but chained to our social media accounts.** We don't see our friends as often as we should, but we know the ins and outs of every character on our favorite shows.

How do we get out of this mess? What do we do now?

The 30 Day Blackout is where we begin. Blacking out will not be easy. There will be days when you want to throw in the towel. There will be tantrums and arguments and more than a little bargaining. But I have walked hundreds of families through the Blackout. I know its power. It is the quickest and most effective method to get out of pain and into a well-functioning family.

Childhood is fleeting. It's over before you know it, and your children don't have any time to waste. Their brains are forming as you read this. Their nervous systems are creating pathways that will be used over and over again throughout their lives. We're running out of time. **They're running out of time.** I know it sounds impossible, I know it won't be easy, but you *can* do this. *They* can do this. And I promise you, it's worth it.

Are you ready to try? Then let's get going.

What's Going on?

Did you know that Steve Jobs, founder of Apple, wouldn't let his own children be exposed to handheld electronic devices, such as his company's iPhone or iPad? In a New York Times article[1] in 2010, he famously told Nick Bilton, the journalist interviewing him, "We limit how much technology our kids use at home."

Bill Gates, Microsoft founder and billionaire, spoke of smartphones and technology use by children to *The Mirror* in June of 2018[2], "You're always looking at how it can be used in a great way—homework and staying in touch with friends—and also where it has gotten to excess... We don't have cellphones at the table when we are having a meal, we didn't give our kids cellphones until they were 14 and they complained other kids got them earlier."

Many tech giants are sending their children to The Waldorf School of the Peninsula[3] in Washington, a school famous for its low to no-tech policies, yet widely held to be one of the most desirable schools.

What do you think they know that you don't? Why are they opting for a traditional, low-tech childhood for their children?

A private school near Sydney, Australia, recently removed iPads from its campus after having used the tablets in place of textbooks for five years. They found the devices to be distracting and that the students were actually learning *less* than they had been with regular textbooks and standard pen-on-paper note-taking. The students themselves said they preferred hard-copy textbooks, and the principal said they used more senses when searching for information in a physical book.[4]

Dr. Marcus-Quinn, a lecturer in Technical Communication and Instructional Design at the University of Limerick in Ireland (where use of iPads in the classroom has been on the rise), said that research around the globe shows that "crucial skills such as the ability to empathize and critically analyze texts may be compromised by a shift to reading texts on tablets."[5]

The impact on children's health is considered serious enough that both the American Academy of Pediatrics and the Canadian Paediatric Society have established public health guidelines around it. These are the same places that recommend bicycle helmets and car seats for children.

Jenny Radesky, MD, FAAP, lead author on several policy statements for the American Academy of Pediatrics, said, "Families should proactively think about their children's media use and talk with children about it, because too much media use can mean that children don't have enough time during the day to play, study, talk, or sleep."[6]

The Journal of Public Health[7] published a study showing a dose-dependent association between metabolic syndrome and screen time in adolescents. That means the more time your teenager spends in front of a screen, the greater his or her chance of developing metabolic syndrome (a group of risk factors that raises the chance of developing heart disease, diabetes, stroke, and premature death, among other things). The results found this connection present independent of exercise, meaning that if your child is an athlete and you think that offsets the risks incurred from playing video games for hours every day, it does not. **Exercise does not cancel out screen time** in health risk factors.

This same study cites the well-known relationship between television viewing and a slew of negative consequences for kids, stating, "Television viewing has also been linked to a number of other important public health issues in youth including violent and aggressive acts, initiation of early sexual behaviors, body self-image issues and substance use and abuse. Excessive computer and video game use has been associated with many of the same health and social problems."

How much more information do we need? How many studies do we have to read? How many doctors, researchers, and teachers will tell us we have a problem before we believe them?

Many phones now have a screen/digital health tool. Why is that? Why would phone manufacturers and cell carriers take that step? Could it be that they are taking seriously the consequences of scrolling page after page, watching video after video, spending inordinate amounts of time on phones, tablets, computers, video games, and other electronic gadgets? What are they concerned about?

We could be cynical and say that limiting screen time is a hot topic and being talked about almost everywhere, from major news outlets and national programs to articles in local newspapers. Fearing their inevitable decline, companies decide to regulate themselves before someone else does it for them. The case against them is building and they don't want to get caught unprepared.

Regardless of what their true motivation is, the Do Not Disturb feature on phones is a useful tool, and we should utilize it.

Here's the truth as I see it, coming from a family therapist who has successfully counseled hundreds of families. **Screens come between us.** They interrupt the traditional methods of communication between people. You can't watch a screen and look directly into someone's eyes at the same time.

Our children are not being nurtured and encouraged as much as they need, and certainly not as much as they deserve. Many of them are being raised by screens. Some parents are so overwhelmed and stressed that they unintentionally default to handing their kids off to the care of a glowing, handheld babysitter.

Technology has usurped not only our children's education but also their playtime. Sadly, it limits both their creativity and their imaginations, as well as their sensory and motor development outside the muscles in their thumbs.

Let's be clear. Lots of things can come between parents and children. Their own natures and personalities,

31

hectic schedules, and traumatic events can drive us apart. Serious issues like illness, physical distance, and military deployment can widen the gap. And not for just parents and children, but also spouses, partners, family, and friends. But in today's culture, what primarily comes between people is media or entertainment of some sort. When you try to talk to your partner, do they immediately look at you and make eye contact, or do they finish the text they're writing first? Do they even hear you the first time you call their name? When you talk to your teenager, do they have to remove their ear buds before they can answer you? Or is it easier to just text them from across the room?

Relationships require attention. If a friend gave you a potted plant for your birthday, and you watered it once and placed it in front of a window, what do you think would happen? It would be all right for a little while—it has water and sunlight, after all. But the thing about plants is that they need water more than once, and too much sun can be just as harmful as not enough. What the plant needs is your attention. Remove it from the sun when the leaves look scorched. Water it when the top of the soil is dry. Prune it in winter. Re-plant it if it outgrows its pot.

That plant is your child. Your husband. Your friend. Your sister. They do not need a phone, or a video game console, or a tablet. **They need you.**

If you were born before 1988, you probably remember a time without cell phones. You might even remember when many homes did not have air conditioning, forcing the entire family outside in warm weather to try to catch a breeze. Children in previous generations knew where all the kids in the neighborhood were by seeing the house with the bicycles piled up in the front yard. Maybe you used a landline telephone (wonderful technology) to call your friends; you were talking to them, hearing their voice and allowing them to hear yours, using inflection and reading someone else's tone. You were honing your social skills without even realizing it. Your parents may have worked late, but in most cases, once they were home, they were home—not working, checking emails, talking to coworkers, or busily putting out fires at the office.

> ### Boundaries
>
> *Think of boundaries as your personal border. They keep private what you want to be private and show to the world what you want to share. They help keep you safe by keeping dangerous things out and vulnerable parts of you in.*
>
> *You decide who is allowed into your personal border and who is not. You decide what is available for public consumption and what should be shared with only a select few.*
>
> *Boundaries are the guardians at the gate.*

Workaholics have always existed and there will always be professions that require a person to be on call or reachable at any moment. But what is disturbing about today's workplace is that it is not just the life-and-death professions that expect 24/7 availability. It is the graphic designer being asked at eleven o'clock at night how the project is coming. It's the personal assistant being called repeatedly during a ballgame on a Saturday afternoon. It's the administrator who can't enjoy her daughter's baby shower because her phone won't quit dinging.

It is wonderful to be in contact with people over great distances. I have loved ones all over the country, and I am grateful for the ability to talk to and communicate with them. Sending pictures of the kids to my family with my phone is an amazing ability. **But even adults need boundaries around technology.**

Years ago, I was spending the evening with a friend. Cell phones had recently grown in popularity but not so much that everyone had one yet. It was still considered rude to take out a phone at the table, so I had left mine in my purse (notice today how many people set their phone on the table next to their plate so they can see it at all times). We were chatting and making plans when my phone rang. I groaned, unhappy to be interrupted. I said something about not wanting to talk and being irritated by the phone, and my friend said something I've never forgotten.

"That phone is there for *your* convenience. Don't answer it if you don't want to."

My convenience. What a novel concept! I didn't have to answer if I didn't want to.

This is what we've lost sight of today. We are there for our phones, not the other way around. We have become slaves to notifications, Twitter feeds, and Instagram likes. Instead of allowing these things to serve us, **we are serving them**.

I have a friend who will text me, and if I don't text back within three minutes, she will call me. If I don't answer, she'll call again. People want instant communication and many feel anxiety when they don't get it. They worry something is wrong; they wonder if their friend is mad at them; their mind concocts outrageous stories of why someone is away from their phone. The truth is usually very simple: a battery was dead or they left their phone in the car. But some people will take great offense at not being immediately responded to and will even become angry when they feel ignored.

This is a problem because we are seeking some kind of connection through social media and texting, but never feeling fully sated at the limited connection we do receive. It's like expecting a feast and being given a breath mint. Of course, we're disappointed!

It's easy to see the link between overuse of technology and depression and anxiety. When used properly, technology, and the screens that go with it, can be a useful tool to help you with various aspects of your life. When used improperly, it gets in the way of what we really want. For many of us, that's solid friendships, fulfilling relationships, and healthy families.

This can look like a cycle of reaching out to someone because we crave connection, feeling rebuffed even if we aren't truly rejected, then feeling angry disproportionately to the situation because we are starved for connection. Imagine not eating for three days, mustering up the strength to beg a friend for food, then arriving at her house only to find out she forgot you were coming and the doors are locked. How would that make you feel? Angry? Disappointed? Rejected? *Forgotten?*

If that's how you feel as an adult, can you imagine how much more alienating technology can be for a small child?

The sight and sound stimulation of our screens causes delays in children's basic developmental milestones. Our children are being exposed to more violence than ever before through the news, TV programs, and video games, which can put them in a state of constant adrenaline rush, a stress on both their minds and bodies. Children are not developmentally capable of managing the adrenaline and sorting out the real from the virtual, and their bodies certainly do not know the difference.

Have you ever watched a scary movie and felt your heart racing? Have you felt frightened? Nervous? Anxious or excited? You are experiencing the action in the movie as if it is happening to you, at least somewhat.

This doesn't happen to everyone. Some people watch what is happening and are able to maintain their composure throughout the experience. Other people are affected at a visceral level. I have a close friend who has a very vivid imagination and a frighteningly clear memory. She still remembers scenes from a scary movie she saw when she was seven, and she gets so involved in the books she's reading and the movies she watches that she has become very selective with what she allows into her imagination, which consequently impacts her nervous system.

It's a good idea to know where you are on this scale of detached to overly identifying. It will help you to manage your own responses to stimuli as well as recognize your children's levels of reaction. That same friend who feels like she is living every movie she watches has found great success with yoga and meditation. One of her children is the same way, and luckily she was able to spot it in him when he was very young and keep him from seeing things he would never be able to forget.

That rush that you feel when you play an intense video game, that fear you feel when the bad guy is closing in on the hero, that's adrenaline. It's released from the adrenal glands, small glands that sit atop your kidneys and control your body's responses to stress, among other things. Two-thousand years ago, two-hundred years ago, even fifty years ago, humans felt fear when there was actual danger. This adrenaline response is helpful in the sense that it gives you the boost you need to escape a dangerous situation. It gives you the energy to run away from a predator, the strength to swim out of a raging river, the fearlessness to fight invaders. It gave hunters that burst of power to chase down prey for food, even if they hadn't eaten in days. It gave—and still gives—mothers the courage to save their babies from a stampede—or oncoming traffic.

Adrenaline is necessary to a healthy-functioning body. Problems arise when we feel a rush of adrenaline that is *not* followed by a burst of intense physical activity. Thousands of years ago, if a wolf was chasing a man through the forest, he could scramble up a tree or into a cave for safety. He burned off the adrenaline so it wasn't coursing aimlessly through his veins, wreaking havoc on his nervous and endocrine systems.

Today, the wolf is your boss emailing you when you're lying in bed and you just have to check it. Adrenaline rushes, but you don't climb a tree to get away. You lie in bed, typing on your phone or laptop, losing sleep and ignoring your partner. Maybe you get up and walk to the kitchen table. Hardly enough activity to offset the enormous adrenaline dump that just took place.

Humans today have the same bodies, systems, and functions that humans had thousands of years ago. Society and technology are changing faster than our bodies are adapting to those changes. Therefore, we have to be caregivers of our own bodies and minds and protect our own nervous systems from the constant onslaught of perceived danger.

To make matters worse, once the adrenaline wears off, we plummet into listlessness and/or anxiety. Post-adrenaline spike, many people will feel lethargic, emotional, weepy, hungry, and impossible to please.

Sound familiar?

As adults, we often text and email instead of talk on the phone or in person. Often, we are using multiple screens at once—watching TV or a computer while using a tablet or phone. I have known husbands and wives to text reminders to one another while sitting in the same room together! These items that are here for our convenience are ruling our lives. And if this is true for us as adults, how much truer is it for our children? This interaction with screens and technology is having a profound and lasting impact on our children's physical, mental, emotional, social, and academic development.

Clinical research clearly shows there is a link between developmental and academic disorders and too much screen time, yet children continue to experience unrestricted and often unsupervised screen time without parental controls. Just as we teach a child to ride a bicycle and care for their physical safety by teaching them to wear a helmet and watch for traffic, we MUST teach children how to safely navigate technology, to warn them of the pitfalls, and to protect them from predators and trauma.

Screen Time
Any activity that happens in front of a screen. Watching television—live or recorded, movies, YouTube, video games, anything on a computer, anything done on a phone or tablet.

We are trading a shared reality for a virtual reality, and it's robbing us of relationships and the connection we long for—and need—in order to thrive. A generation is growing up right before our eyes that doesn't understand true connection because so few of us are truly connecting.

Screens aren't just messing with their connections, but also with their expectations. In an article in Psychology Today[8] by Liraz Margalit, Ph.D., she explains how screen-based kids' games give instant gratification. They push a button and get a smiley face. They get the right answer and there are fireworks. It programs children, particularly those at the early developmental phase (1-3 years of age), to want rewards instantly.

But real life doesn't work like that. Sometimes you have to wait for food to be ready, or you can't go where you want to go at the exact moment you want to go there. But children programmed to believe rewards should be frequent and instantaneous have gotten used to a regular hit of dopamine, the reward chemical that releases when we feel pleasure, and they can become dependent on its regular release. They will prefer its instant gratification to the slower pace of real life.

The journal *Pediatrics* published an article in 2016 that said, "Because of their immature symbolic, memory, and attentional skills, infants and toddlers cannot learn from traditional digital media as they do from interactions with caregivers, and they have difficulty transferring that knowledge to their 3-dimensional experience."[9]

In layman's terms, babies and toddlers do not learn as well from a flat screen as they do from real life and real interactions. Touching objects with their hands and learning their shape and weight and texture; learning these things with a person they know and trust.

The Kaiser Family Foundation regularly studies the impact of screens on children, and their surveys find that on average, American children spend seven and a half hours per day in front of some sort of screen entertainment.[10] Seven and a half! Imagine what that is doing to the brains of those children.

In contrast, the National Institutes of Health[11] reports that the average child spends only 25 minutes per day reading. That's 18 times more television, video games, and computer use than reading. **Eighteen times more!**

Countless children fall asleep with their phones or tablets each night. Some children in my office say the only reason they get off their devices is because the battery dies.

That's dependency.

If they are on a screen in virtual reality, then they are not bonding with people in *actual* reality. This lack of true experience, both with nature and with other people, can delay mental development. That includes academic performance, behavior regulation, impulse control, and emotional stability.

With all this screen time, many children struggle to regulate their own emotions. It seems they are more bonded to their screens than to other people. They do not have an opportunity to get to know themselves and to know what they are feeling or why, much less work through those feelings.

> **Virtual Reality**
>
> *We all know what reality is. It's what's true and actually here. Virtual means nearly or almost, meaning virtual reality is almost real. Almost, but not quite.*

People of all ages feel a broad range of emotions–feelings come and go on a regular basis. But children with too much screen time lose their ability to experience this naturally. They can get "stuck" at a young emotional age, falling emotionally and developmentally behind their chronological age. That means an 11-year-old might be acting more like an 8-year-old. If you see a child acting very young for their age, this may be the reason.

What I'm seeing in my practice are children who exhibit signs of social anxiety in simple face-to-face interactions, children who cannot maintain eye contact, and children who are unfocused and cannot pay attention for more than 30 seconds at a time.

It makes sense when you think about how a screen works. You look at a screen but it does not look back at you. Children who spend too much time in front of screens become uncomfortable with eye contact or even being observed by a live person. Screens do not talk back to you naturally, but only with simulated, programmed responses, causing kids to be uncomfortable with making conversation where they have to act and react spontaneously in real time, not with the slow deliberation texting allows.

My observations are consistent with that of clinicians all over the world who work with children and families. You can't turn on the news without seeing a new report on the damage screens are doing to our children. We are approaching a worldwide crisis of epic proportions. If a child is not outside—walking, playing, stimulating the five senses in a natural setting—it can lead to persistent body sensations such as shaking, accelerated breathing and heart rate, and a general feeling of uneasiness.

While the long-term effects of this chronic state of stress in a developing child are currently unknown, we do know that chronic stress in adults results in a weakened immune system, a variety of diseases and disorders, and even early death. I don't want my child to become another number in the research, a statistic detailing the collateral damage of technology and the never-ceasing march of progress.

I want better for my child, and I know you do, too.

So now you know what the problem is, but what do you do about it? I'm so glad you asked. The next page has a list of questions you can answer to determine whether or not there is too much screen time in your child's life. Once you've identified it, we'll start working on solving the problem.

If you're wondering if your child has too much screen time, take this quiz.

1. Is your child's behavior unmanageable?
2. Do you feel you cannot reach your child?
3. Does your child lose his temper or become angry when you ask him to turn off the screen or game?
4. Does it seem your child is lost in space? In their own world? Not living in reality?
5. Does it seem everyone in your home is doing their own thing? Everyone in their own room on separate screens? Or multiple screens at once?
6. Is it nearly impossible to get everyone around the dinner table for a simple meal without screens all around you?
7. Does your child seem overly anxious? Depressed?
8. Is your child having a difficult time sleeping or getting good rest?
9. Does your child seem easily frightened? Easily startled?
10. Is it difficult for you to get your children to want to play outside?
11. Does your child seem isolated and you don't know why?
12. Does your child seem distracted and have a difficult time prioritizing family time?
13. Is your family having a difficult time connecting?

If you answered YES to at least 3 questions, congratulations.

You understand there's a problem.

You've picked up this book to look for a solution.

You're on the right track.

And it's important to know something before we go any further.

It's Not Your Fault.

And You Are Not Alone.

Interview with Leanna Rae, MSW

Synergetic Play Therapist
Kid's Brain Tree, Fort Worth, TX

as told to Elizabeth Adams

Leanna is a therapist and Simplicity Parenting Coach who heads up Kid's Brain Tree in Fort Worth, Texas. She recently led several families in her clinic through a 30 Day Blackout. In addition to the usual 30 days, they completed a preparation week designed for the parents to notice and observe their families' use of technology, as well as their own.

The majority of participating families discovered they were using more technology than they realized. Once they added everything up—the television, phones, tablets, computers, and video games—they saw it was much more pervasive than they had initially thought.

The other focus of the prep week was to discover each family's "why," both individually and as a collective whole. What were their goals? Why did they want to do a Blackout and what did they hope to achieve through it?

"The idea was that if they didn't have a solid 'why,' they could abandon ship more easily," says Leanna.

Most of the kids in the clinic are dealing with behavioral issues like ADHD—lots of attention problems and sibling relationship issues—and fewer cases of cutting and suicidal ideation.

Leanna specifically noticed Thomas, her own 8-year-old son's relationship with his 4-year-old brother. "He was the one I was continually having to coach. He didn't have the capacity or inner quietness to have patience," says Leanna. "You can't lecture patience into a child."

What Leanna noticed with her own children, and what the parents of the children in her clinic noticed as well, was that all the children were sleeping better. They also increased their ability to retain information—enough that their teachers noticed and commented to the parents. Even though it was the end of the school year, grades went up and the children reported understanding things better and being less confused in school. Parents said they were repeating themselves less.

"It was easier to get their attention. They didn't have to prompt them as much."

Parents also reported a lot more talking. Conversations were deeper and more personal, and many of them would not have occurred without the Blackout.

The most universal difference? "Creativity went sky high," says Leanna proudly.

This is a common side effect of the Blackout. Kids began drawing, painting, writing, playing differently, engaging differently, and accessing their imaginations in ways they hadn't before.

In Leanna's own family, eating patterns changed. Her son Thomas has always had a strong sweet tooth, constantly requesting treats and always wanting more sugar than his parents had allotted. During the Blackout, his sugar cravings decreased drastically.

"We were not trying to focus on sugar or change anything at all," says Leanna. It was just a pleasant side effect.

Midway through the Blackout was Easter Sunday with all its attendant festivities and sugar-coated treats. Leanna was dreading it, hoping to avoid the usual begging and crying involved when she denied sugar. Thomas would surprise her.

"He had two pieces of candy and he said, 'That's enough, I'm good. I'm going to go play.' He didn't ask for it at all after that," says a stunned Leanna.

Her hypothesis? "The decreased stress internally affects the microbiome in the gut resulting in fewer cravings."

Thomas is still regulating his own sugar cravings, months after weaning himself off sweets. Several other parents at the clinic with kids on the ADD/ADHD spectrum reported significantly reduced sugar and carb cravings in their children.

After observing her kids through the Blackout, Leanna has come to the conclusion that Thomas is more sensitive to technology than her other children. He was also the one that she noticed the greatest changes in, especially with his younger brother.

"That relationship has done a complete 180," she says.

The other families in the clinic reported the same thing. Across the board, sibling relationships improved— less challenge, competitiveness, and fighting, with more nurturing and collaboration. Even when the kids weren't playing together, they would sometimes read next to each other, just enjoying one another's company.

The kids slept better and were more rested, and consequently easier to get going in the morning with smoother routines. Children were more engaged and more responsive; they blossomed before their parents' eyes.

One child in the group did say he got headaches during the Blackout. Leanna and his parents believe he likely had them all along, but his constant distraction on screens blinded him to his own physical state. They can address it appropriately now that his nervous system is regulating.

It is Leanna's hope to lead more group Blackouts in the future, some done in the original format, others with additions. For example, a Blackout that focuses on gratitude, or nutrition, or parenting. She has seen first-hand that everything is connected and feels strongly about understanding the root cause of a problem and not just treating the symptoms.

Leanna remarks of therapists in general, "It is really to our detriment if we keep making behavioral plans without dealing with the source of the problem."

She wants to get the child's nervous system regulated, get a baseline, then gradually add in technology and see where the child's capacity and tolerance for technology is. Each child will be different.

Just as Leanna noticed her son's heightened sensitivity and low tolerance to the little screen time he was exposed to, so must parents learn what their child can and cannot handle and how it is affecting his/her nervous system, behavior, emotions, and diet.

Cara Soto, BCBA and Director of Behavioral Services at Kid's Brain Tree, says, "Behavior is only scary if you don't have a plan."

It's become Leanna's personal motto. Leanna also recommends that before leading a group through the Blackout, that clinicians do it on their own with their families. In fact, it's not a bad idea for parents as well.

"Some parents need to start on their own before the kids. Maybe the first two weeks on their own, then add the kids to the Blackout."

When one parent is not fully on board with the Blackout, it can be a burden on the other parent in the family. If one is dealing with all the difficulties kids bring to this scenario, along with adjusting their own screen time, adding on a surly partner who doesn't want to give up his/her favorite leisure activity is like pushing a boulder uphill. They can feel like an additional child, but this one can't be sent to their room when they are petulant and difficult. For this reason, Leanna suggests the parents begin the Blackout on their own first and become comfortable with it themselves, then bring in the children later if the parents suspect this will be a problem.

Her advice for getting through the Blackout (and other hard things), both as a mother and a clinician? "Remember that a meltdown is not a teachable moment."
Well said.

2

Where Do We Go from Here?

Is there a solution for this crisis? In a word, yes. Using screens got you here. Removing them will get you out.

I'm not here to make anyone feel guilty. We live in a society that actively encourages the excessive use of technology. You can hardly ask someone a question without them asking you if you looked it up on Google yet. We don't remember phone numbers anymore because our phones do it for us. If we're not watching the latest "it" series, people look at us like we're crazy.

We take photos at meals and live Tweet at concerts. We have social media profiles where we share more information with strangers than we would tell our grandparents. We use our phones for nearly everything: email, taking photos, texting, directions, music, watching videos! Sometimes it seems like their least used function is calling people.

An enormous amount of money is spent on marketing phones, tablets, laptops, and the apps we use on them. Highly trained researchers study you and your buying habits, then put that information to use. You have been bombarded with images, catchy songs, enviable storylines, and commercials filled with beautiful people doing amazing things. It's no surprise that you bought what they were selling.

Western culture has fallen down the rabbit hole of technology and is dragging all of us with it. You are not at fault for listening to "experts" who told you that your children needed to be using technology sooner so they would be competitive in the workplace. You are not at fault for wanting your child to feel like he belongs. You never intended to harm your children, and **this is not your fault**.

This is what society told you to do. This is what the experts recommended. The voices of dissent have been few and quiet.

That is what this book is for. To once and for all dispel the notion that giving screens to children is a good idea. Even if it's educational. Even if it makes them happy for the time they're on it. Even if people tell you kids need it to be smarter or more successful. The research says otherwise.

I'll say again, I'm not here to make you feel guilty. I'm here to stand beside you in the trenches and find a way out of this problem.

We've all had rough days when we just don't have the patience to handle our kids, especially if they are having a rough day, too. I know—I have four children of my own—I get it. The lure of tagging off to entertainment is strong. If you do this once in a while (no more than once a week), it isn't so bad. It's when this is the norm, when every afternoon after school is spent in front of the television or the computer, when weekends are spent sitting in separate rooms on separate devices, that it becomes a serious problem.

I am not anti-technology. Okay, I am anti-technology for babies, toddlers, and young children. Here's a good rule of thumb: **If your children are small enough to be carried, they shouldn't be using screens.**

Technology has amazing power to bring us together if we use it the way it was intended—to be a *supplement* to our lives and not the *purpose* of our lives. We should use phones to communicate with each other, not to ignore each other. It should make our jobs easier and our work more efficient so we can spend *more* time enjoying life with our loved ones; it shouldn't be an excuse to never really leave work and be available to our bosses and coworkers every moment of every day.

Let's put technology back in its place. It is our servant, not the other way around. Remember that. **You own the technology. It does not own you.**

After years of treating children with a host of behavioral problems, I've realized connection is the missing ingredient. What if parents whose children were suffering from these behavioral ailments turned everything off for 30 days? What if these families could unplug from technology and plug in to each other? What do you think would happen?

The 30 Day Blackout is now what I recommend to the majority of my clients who come to me with children who have behavioral problems. As you will see, the results are truly remarkable.

So how does it work? It's challenging to execute but very simple to understand.

If parents came into my office, my first and most pressing question after my traditional intake would be, "How much screen time?" I would follow that with, "That includes everything with a screen, including tablets, phones, computers, TV, and video games?"

I would typically glance up from my clipboard and see them fidgeting, with an uncomfortable, slightly agitated look in their eyes. I would likely detect an expression of caught-red-handed, to which I would respond by looking down at my notes and adding up the screen time they have detailed based on their child's schedule. Over the years, I have learned to multiply this number by two or three because I have come to realize that most parents who come to see me really have no idea how much screen time their children are exposed to because they rarely place any limits around it or don't enforce those they do place.

At this point, I've had perfectly intelligent fathers ask me, "What about TV?" as if the television somehow gets a free pass. I simply ask, "Is the TV a screen?" And then they sort of chuckle.

Sometimes they don't.

Research in the field of mental health shows that the quality of the bond between a child and their primary caregiver affects their lifelong ability to connect with others. That means their relationship with their parents, grandparents, nanny, babysitter, etc., will influence the kind of partners they choose, the marriages they have, the friendships they maintain (or don't maintain) and the relationships they have with their own children if they have them.

Children (and adults) are hardwired to connect with those around them. They are either invested in real reality, or our new option called virtual reality.

Reality is an experience using the five senses— something that grounds you enough that you know where and who you are. Virtual reality means "almost real," and can cause derealization (being unaware of reality) and depersonalization (being unsure of who you are). So if children are wired to connect, and they are also living the majority of their time in virtual reality, what happens?

Attachment disorders, behavioral problems, ADD/ADHD, lack of social skills, academic deficiencies, difficulty concentrating, shortened attention spans, ticks, manic states, hyperarousal, hypoarousal, and in extreme cases, psychosis.

True connection needs cannot be met through the "almost real" experience of virtual reality. Children will remember best their experiences that utilized all or most of their five senses. Experiences that grounded them in reality. But children won't remember their best day of television or video games.

Think back to your own childhood. Did you play a lot of video games? Watch a lot of television? Did you have a Gameboy or similar device?

How do you feel about the time you spent doing those things? Was it just a little bit and no big deal? Did you do it with friends and it was a bonding activity? Or do you barely recall it, just a hazy memory of watching TV after school or playing video games and lounging on a bean bag in somebody's basement?

Was it a good use of your time? Are you happy that was how you grew up, or do you wish it had been different? Would it have been better to have been involved in a sport? Maybe something musical like chorus or band or dance. You could have joined the debate team, or drill team, model UN, the chess club, science club, art club. You could have learned to paint, learned to cook, learned a foreign language, studied for your SATs. You could have gotten a job and earned money to buy a car, to put towards college tuition, or to take an epic post-graduation trip.

Take a moment and think about it. Think about how you used your time growing up. Think about how much of that time was in front of a screen. Now really ask yourself, and tell the truth, what you think about that. Was it time well spent? Or was it time wasted?

When I was a little girl, I watched a lot of TV. As a latchkey kid, the TV was my babysitter. To this day I can remember the list of shows I would watch day after day. In the morning it was the news, followed by *The Price Is Right* and *Let's Make a Deal*. Then around lunchtime it was *Guiding Light, As the World Turns, One Life to Live* and *General Hospital*, followed by *The Jeffersons, All In the Family, Wheel of Fortune* and the news again. In hindsight, I wish I could have all that wasted time back, all the time I spent in front of my electronic babysitter. I wish I had done something productive, like learned to cook or read more books. I wish I had spent more time with my friends.

In the spirit of honesty, I will tell you that all that time in front of the television was detrimental to my physical and mental health. For decades, I had trouble focusing for more than short periods of time, and even then I had to be interested in the topic. It seems to me that most adults can make themselves listen to something they don't want to hear if they feel the need; like a child learns to sit still in church or in the classroom, they take those lessons into adulthood. I could not do that. What I considered to be my "one-track-mind" made me a poor listener and was a source of constant frustration for those close to me. My inability to be in the moment with the current conversation meant I would comment on the earlier topic long after the conversation had moved on, often confusing our communication. I was not really participating in the conversation—not in real time.

I was out of tune with my own body and spent years struggling with unhealthy eating habits accompanied by dysfunctional relationships. My energy was either on or off and very little in between.

Was all of this the fault of television? No. That would be too simple. Remember I had an alcoholic father and a passive mother, but the television certainly didn't help. In fact, it was a very visible cry for help, had there been anyone around to recognize it. I spent hours watching other people because I needed people in my own life. I spent hours watching families because I needed my own family. I watched the news in an effort to connect with a community I didn't truly feel a part of. I had a curious mind, but no one to nurture it.

A television, or a tablet, or a phone or a computer, cannot love you back. It cannot be your mom. It cannot have a conversation with you, it cannot offer empathy and kindness. It is just a screen, and a poor substitute for the love and care we all truly desire.

Before you feel sorry for me, know that I now have a healthy relationship with technology, with food, and with the people in my life. I have worked very hard to achieve peace in my life, and it is because of my own experience that I care so deeply about this issue and why I feel qualified to speak out on this topic. **I was the child you are trying to heal now.** I was the child I see in my office every day.

And I am now a healthy, happy adult with a loving husband, four wonderful children, and family and friendships I can rely on.

Looking back at my childhood, I am grateful I had a roof over my head, food on the table, and friends to play with. But due to my life's circumstances, there wasn't a lot of connecting going on in my home. Unfortunately, back then no one near me knew a way out of the disconnection, the fighting, and the chaos. They simply didn't see a lost little girl sitting in front of a television, rather, they saw the "Walking TV Guide" as they used to call me. But I was a little Walking TV guide who was desperate for someone to see me, hear me, celebrate and delight in me.

The point I'm making is this: while I do remember in agonizing detail the daily TV schedule of my youth, I have no fond or lasting memories of all the time I spent in front of the screen. There may have been an occasional movie where I felt the presence of my family around me, but I mostly felt pawned off.

My story is not your story, but I imagine you have your own version of neglect or loneliness or loss, either as the child or as the parent. By picking up this book you are admitting there is a problem in your family, and you are ready to do something to address it.

When I introduce the concept of the 30 Day Blackout to a child or family they look at me like I have lost my mind. Then I look back at them with confidence because I know in my heart I am offering them a proven alternative to achieve what they really want and need, which is true connection. And that need simply cannot be fulfilled by a screen, no matter how much we try.

Taking Stock

So, in a shame-free zone, it's time to take stock and get honest with where things currently stand. If you were my client sitting in my office, I would take a full history on your child, a timeline of his or her life. I would pay special attention to any traumas the child may have suffered, either real or imaginary, because there is no such thing as a universal trauma, as the experience of an event is based on perception. Every person does not experience the same feelings in similar scenarios. One person's adventure can be another's traumatic experience.[12]

Take the classic *Rudolph the Red-Nosed Reindeer* Christmas movie, for example. My oldest child thought the Abominable Snow Monster was the scariest thing she had ever seen in her life. My son at that same age, on the other hand, thought the Abominable Snow Monster was hilarious. Two different children, two different perceptions. One was frightened, the other laughing.

The same is true with video games and television shows.

Some children simply have no desire to sit in front of a screen all day. I believe those children, for the most part, have parents setting healthy limits and examples for them. These children have too many other connection-based, interactive activities to keep their attention. Their screen time is the dessert of their lives, not the main course.

Other children, far too many in our culture today, are on their devices from the time they get up until they go to sleep, missing out on the true wonders of childhood and the experiences and relationships they need in order to grow and thrive.

If you were my client, during our second session, I would facilitate an interactive session where I observe the relationship between you and your child in order to understand how you interact. I would give you instructions on what I call "play cards." These depict a combination of activities such as parent-led play, child-led play, building structures with blocks, cleanup time, and playing a game together. You get the idea.

I would take notes on simple questions: How much eye contact is your child giving you at home? How much push-back? Is your child compliant or strong-willed? Is your child showing signs of anxiety? Are they shut down? Angry? Defiant? Are you as the parent distracted or present? Are you able to put all your concerns and worries aside to be present with your child and simply connect? What discipline style do you use?

I would then lead you in an activity I refer to as "Color My Mountain,"[13] where I talk about how we are going to climb a mountain together. I would draw two mountains on an art easel, side by side, and ask you and your child to pick five colors, one for each of the following feelings.

- Happy
- Sad
- Mad
- Worried
- Scared

I would then say, "Imagine the two of you are climbing this mountain together. I want you to think about how much of your mountain feels happy, how much of your mountain feels sad, and how much of your mountain feels mad, worried, or scared."

I would have you pick out one more feeling that you often feel and add that to the colors in your hand. Some children will pick feelings like confused, bored, or lonely. Parents many times will select feelings like busy, overwhelmed, or stressed.

At the end of your quiet time coloring together, I would have you take turns asking each other what makes you feel happy, sad, mad, worried, and scared, along with the last feeling you chose. This teaches active listening skills.

For example:

"Sarah, what makes you happy?"

Sarah answers, "What makes me happy is when I get to spend time with you, our dog, when we all eat dinner together as a family, and when we go out for ice cream."

I coach the parent to simply repeat back, "So what I'm hearing you say is what really makes you happy is when you get to spend time with me, our dog, when we all eat dinner together as a family, and when we go out for ice cream. Is that right?"

The child agrees and the parent asks, "Is there anything else?"

This is what I call "Birdie Talk," which is where each parent simply repeats back to the child what they heard the child say. This helps the child feel acknowledged, or what I call "seen, heard, celebrated, and delighted in." This is what we all want to experience in our important relationships in life. **Sadly, many of us have forgotten how this feels, if we ever truly knew.**

After this session with you and your child, where the child has experienced your full attention in a creative, play-based setting for 45 minutes, I will ask the two of you to discuss what you each liked the most and least in your play time together. You will look each other in the eyes and have a simple, honest conversation.

I cannot tell you how many times I've received a note or email from a parent saying something along the lines of, "On the way out of your office today my son told me this was the best day of his life. We have been spending so much time doing activities (school, ballet, gymnastics, athletics, vacations, church) that we forgot the basics of true connection. I forgot how simple it can be. Thank you!"

Whenever possible, I repeat the same play-based assessment[14] with the other parent in our third session, regardless of whether or not the parents are married or divorced. I do this to give the child the same undivided attention with both parents. I want to see how the relationship is different and if the behavior changes from parent to parent. Plus, I want to help you both slow down, look your child in the eyes, and give that child the time and attention they need to thrive.

In our next session, I would sit down with both parents to collaborate on a treatment plan that I call the Mountain Method. In this session, we decide where at the bottom of the mountain we are, and what we want to achieve at the top. We won't go into details on the whole Mountain Method in this book, but the first step is usually the 30 Day Blackout. Think of this as base camp at Mount Everest. Still hard to get to, but not the full distance.

Now it's your turn. These are hard questions, and some won't be easy to answer honestly, either because you aren't sure, or because it is painful. But being honest with yourself is the best way to get on the road to recovery and freedom. Pretending there is no problem won't accomplish anything.

No one can see you. No one can read your answers or hear your thoughts. Remember this is a shame-free zone. So, take your time. Really think about your answers.

Where are you at the bottom of your mountain?
Is your child withdrawn?
Are you and your family in separate rooms on your devices, not connecting with each other?
Do you have screens going in multiple rooms of your home?
How are your children feeling? Angry? Defiant? Another emotion?
Are they constantly fighting?
Is it worse when you try to take the screen away?
Do you rely on screens to keep your children quiet while you are driving? Are you pulling your hair out wondering how things got this bad?
Most importantly, are you ready for change?

63

This is what I tell my clients, and it is what I will tell you. This is difficult, but it's worth it. What you will give up is so small compared to what you can gain.

Things you could gain from blacking out:

- Better relationship with your children
- Better relationship with your partner and/or co-parent
- More joy
- More peace of mind
- Time to do what you *really* want to do
- The feeling that you really *know* your child
- Increased creativity
- Increased confidence and self-worth in your children
- Increased confidence in yourself as a parent or caregiver
- Kids who do chores without arguing or even being asked
- Better grades in school
- Better behavior at school
- Better study habits
- Increased interest in physical activities like sports, dance, and playing outside
- Improved friendships for children and adults alike
- Curiosity in your children and yourself
- Higher quality sleep and more of it
- Better overall health for the entire family
- Increased ability to focus

Things you could lose or reduce from Blacking out:

- Tantrums, meltdowns, and outbursts
- Hostility, arguing, and pushback
- Sibling rivalry
- Troublesome behaviors like cutting, stealing, violence, suicidal ideation, bullying, etc.
- Bedtime drama
- Depressed immune systems
- Insomnia or difficulty sleeping—for you and the kids
- Ailments related to lack of sleep
- Hyper, uncontrollable behavior
- Depression
- Anxiety
- Excessive, unmanageable energy that changes focus every minute
- Odd or excessive food cravings
- Various unmanageable compulsions
- Ticks and twitches
- Manic states

I believe the journey will change your life but be warned: this is not an easy road you've chosen. I had a client years ago tell me, "If I have to climb Mount Everest, I want to go with someone who has been there and has climbed it before."

I've been up this mountain before—many, many times. And I have many parents who feel like it saved their children and their families. I will gladly be your guide and walk you through it if you're willing to put in the hard work that the 30 Day Blackout will require.

1. Take an honest look at your child's screen time. How many hours per day are they on some sort of device or screen? Is one device predominantly used? Television more than tablet, for example? Do this for each child in your home.
2. Examine your own screen time. How many hours per day are you on a screen (excluding time at work on calls and computers)? What is your screen of choice? Do this for yourself and any other adults living in your home.
3. Does the idea of a Blackout frighten or bother you? Why?
4. What are you trying to achieve with the Blackout? Solve a specific problem? More peace at home? Be as detailed as possible. Making a list of what you hope to gain and reduce, similar to the one above, can be very motivating.
5. Color your own mountain with your child (or children, one at a time) as described in the beginning of this chapter. Think about where you are now, and where you want to be. Giving a name to your goals and your child's feelings is helpful in understanding your situation as it is and what you hope it will be.

Interview with Wayne

as told to Elizabeth Adams

Wayne is a single dad with a ten-year-old daughter. They started seeing Stacy four years ago when Wayne and his wife went through an extremely high-conflict divorce. Their daughter Caroline didn't have a very solid relationship with her mother, and she took the divorce pretty badly.

They were in and out of therapy for a few years until last autumn when things got desperate. Caroline had thick, blonde hair that she usually wore down and tucked behind her ears. Her teacher noticed something looked off but couldn't put her finger on what. One Wednesday afternoon, Caroline pulled her hair back into a ponytail for gym and that was when her teacher saw the bald spot on the back of her head.

Caroline was old enough not to require help getting ready in the morning. Wayne had no idea that she had been systematically pulling her hair out until she had a large patch missing on the back of her head. Whenever she felt anxious, she would reach up and tug, piece by piece, finding relief in the stinging pull on her scalp and the way the strands would slide through her fingers as she plucked them. She kept the hair she had pulled in the back of her sock drawer, undiscovered until her father got a very disturbing call from his daughter's school.

Once the trichotillomania—the official term for pulling out one's own hair—was discovered, they immediately went back to therapy. Unfortunately, there were more surprises in store.

Caroline was severely depressed and utterly isolated. She had no desire to live any more, and at the age of ten, she was imagining ways to kill herself.

Wayne was deeply disturbed and willing to do whatever was necessary to help his daughter.

"Stacy told me it was time to make some serious changes," says Wayne.

Caroline had had a rough season in her young life. In a relatively short period of time, her mother's house was broken into and nearly everything stolen. Thankfully, Caroline was with Wayne at the time, but it was still incredibly shocking. Then her mother remarried, another massive change in her young life. On top of all of that, Caroline was being bullied in school.

Her parents thought she was coping with all of this relatively well, but the pile of hair in the back of the drawer grew steadily larger.

Enter the Blackout.

Wayne has to stay connected to his phone for work, so it is almost always with him. He also often works from home, so he frequently tagged off to the TV to keep Caroline occupied while he got some work done.

"It's pretty easy to have an electronic babysitter. My parents basically said, 'Go watch TV for a little while and leave me alone,'" Wayne says.

Because it had worked for his parents, Wayne didn't see the problem with doing it with his daughter. Obviously, he would need to do something different. Completely blacking out was not an option for him because his work was done primarily on a computer.

To make the Blackout work for their little family, he compromised. He and his daughter would both turn everything off and put away the phones for a designated amount of time each day. Caroline was experiencing a more complete Blackout, but Wayne really enjoyed those few hours when he was free of devices.

"It was really hard, at first, to put that phone down," says Wayne. But he eventually grew to look forward to it.

"I can't emphasize how powerful it was for me to say I'm going to put all this crap away and go connect with my daughter."

He wasn't the only one feeling the power.

"When Caroline stays away from electronic input and spends her time interacting with people—parents, family, friends, being outside—there is a marked difference in her mental health, no doubt about it."

The family only did a full Blackout for a short time, but they stayed in a Grayout—drastically reduced screen time—for several months and are still doing so today. Now the screens that Caroline is exposed to are limited. Just the television when Wayne is with her—never on her own, and computer games with permission, and often with her father nearby or watching her play, which she enjoys.

The time that had been spent on a phone or in unhealthy video games is now spent in conversation or playing outside with friends. Her hair is growing back, and she is no longer suicidal.

After six months of reducing screen time, they have a new normal. Their daily routine typically follows this pattern: Caroline comes home from school and plays with her friends outside, then comes in around 5:30 and eats dinner with her father. They talk about their days and their upcoming plans and spend 30 minutes to an hour focusing on each other.

Then it's bath time, and afterward they often watch a television show together. They have a handful of favorite programs that are all Wayne-approved and not overstimulating to the nervous system. Sometimes they talk about the plot or the characters, especially if someone is particularly unusual or something odd happens on the show. Other times they just enjoy laughing together and then go to bed. It's less than half an hour of screen viewing, and they make it an activity they can do together.

Caroline no longer plays video games on her own or has her own phone.

"Stacy makes the point that some of these influences are just not good for children. You think, 'Yeah right, it's just a video game,' then you watch what happens after they play and you're like, yeah, this really isn't good for them," Wayne says.

Though he was skeptical at first, he now says they will be in a light Grayout forever. "It was really a transformational thing for us."

3

The Process

The Johnson family was desperate. I could see it in the parents' eyes. Their nine-year-old daughter Maddy, who just a few years ago was a bright, happy, connected child, had now stopped talking. The only way she communicated with them was by grunting or pointing. She had reached a high point of defiance, where the only activity she wanted to engage in was sitting alone in her room playing video games. She refused to talk to anybody.

By the time I met her, she appeared lifeless and unexpressive in every way. Her body language was nearly nonexistent, and I couldn't really see her face because she constantly looked down at the floor. She had been isolating herself in this way for almost two years, and her desperate parents could not understand what was wrong with her, or what had gone wrong in their family. They were hardworking, upper-middle-class people who both had jobs outside the home. Their two other children did not seem to have any of the characteristics Maddy was exhibiting and seemed to be functioning normally. So, what was wrong with their nine-year-old little girl? Where had their Maddy gone?

In my play-based assessment session with Maddy, she displayed helplessness and complete unwillingness to engage in play. This is highly unusual for a child in her play years, which is typically ages 3 to 12. She would occasionally answer with a "yes" or "no" or simply shake her head. She seemed to be in an emotionally constricted, lethargic, mind-numbing depression, with a dulled capacity for life that no one could understand. It was as if she was with us but not really "with us" at all. It was one of the saddest cases of a child responding with a dorsal vagal parasympathetic collapse response due to an overuse of screen time I've ever seen.

What? A dorsal vagal parasympathetic what? What IS that?

Don't tune out, please. This is going to get a little scientific, but I promise it will all make sense. I'll keep it simple.

To have a basic understanding of the nervous system, this is all you need to know.

If you are breathing, you have an active nervous system that contains two elements—a *sympathetic* nervous system, which revs us up, and a *parasympathetic* nervous system that calms us down. There are two branches of the parasympathetic, the ventral and the dorsal. The ventral is when we are in a state of openness that allows us to feel okay in the world. The dorsal is when we have a collapse response.

For example, if a child spends three hours on high adrenaline, running from and shooting at bad guys in a video game, his nervous system may process that as though it is happening in real life. This is a sympathetic activation—blood pumping, heart pounding, cortisol rushing through his veins. Blood pressure rises, sweat glands release, and pupils dilate. All of this stimulates the body's fight or flight response. (Remember the feeling of being chased.)

Then mom turns the video game off, which is equivalent to taking a car traveling at 100 miles per hour and instantly slamming on the brakes. The body reels, the mind panics, just like you would if you were actually running from people trying to shoot you and the bullets suddenly stopped flying.

This massive shift dysregulates the nervous system. And that same child, who moments before was hyper-focused with what seemed like tons of energy, is now slumped down on the sofa, unexpressive, lethargic, and seemingly unable to transition back to real life. This is a child in a collapse response.

There you have it. A dorsal vagal parasympathetic collapse response.

Vulnerable children who have too much screen time are most often in a *hyper*aroused state, exhibiting characteristics of hyperalertness, hypervigilance, and increased heart rate. Some of these children are disassociated, which is a mental process of disconnecting from one's thoughts, feelings, memories, or sense of identity. Many are aggressive with fits of rage. Most are highly irritable, overwhelmed, and anxious. Being defensive and disorganized is also common.

That's what happened to Jake. I saw him for three months. He was argumentative, he went along with nothing, he never had an easy moment. He argued with peers, teachers, everyone. He was defiant and becoming violent. Even being in the same room with him was irritating in the beginning—I could feel his anxiously aggressive energy. He was never invited to birthday parties and had no friends. He was completely unable to regulate his own emotions. To everyone else, this looked like highly irritating behavior and his parents were at the end of their rope.

Jake was *hyperaroused.*

In my experience, it is more typical for boys to be hyperaroused, but it does happen with girls.

Want to guess what my first question was?

"How much screen time?"

Some children who have experienced too much screen time may alternately find themselves in the opposite situation—a *hypo*aroused state not too different from Maddy. Typical symptoms include isolation, lack of motivation, helplessness, lifelessness, lethargy, depression, and disassociation.

What we're looking for is a ventral activation (think post-yoga class) in our nervous systems. This is when we can think logically and clearly. We are able to make conscious choices, initiate eye contact, and display a wide range of emotional expression. When we are in a grounded, ventral state, we are able to notice our breathing and we feel poised. We are able to communicate in a clear manner and our sleep cycles are stable. We are mindful. We are grounded. We feel at ease in the world.

Many children have never felt this in their lives. Many adults haven't either. This is why it's important to understand the basics of the nervous system.

Too much screen time or developmentally inappropriate screen time can keep our children in a constant state of sympathetic activation—they are always being chased. And what is so odd is that if a child sees something he *perceives* as a shock to the system, he will simply want to see it again. The cycle looks something like this:

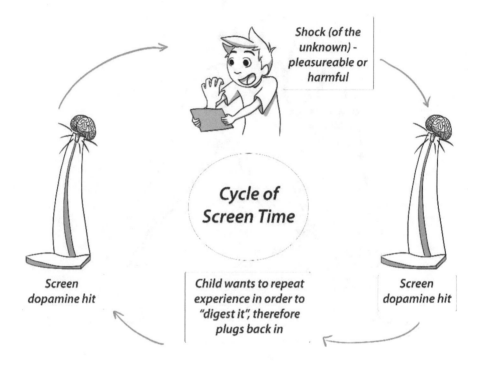

Trauma is anything the nervous system cannot process or integrate. Perception is key, because there is no such thing as universal trauma—remember, everyone doesn't respond to the same events in the same way. It is all based on an individual's perception.

The 30 Day Blackout comes in to take a child out of this cycle of trauma and back into a regulated, natural state. The Blackout becomes the loving parent who knows everyone in the family is going to be mad but realizes it's the best thing for them.

It's good parenting.

At parent consultations, I highly recommend the Blackout to most families, even if they try to persuade me otherwise. There are very few exceptions to the parents' resistance. With Maddy's family, the father tried to convince me that because it was football season, turning off the TV was practically impossible.

To which I replied, "I'll be honest with you. If you are not willing to drastically reduce screen time, I'm not sure how much I can help your family."

Ultimately, the parents have to make the decision. Not all therapists take this "grenade in the lap" approach, but I choose it when I know it will produce immediate results and get a child out of pain as soon as possible.

After the initial shock of thinking about doing the Blackout wore off, I explained some reasonable modifications the family could make. Both Mom and Dad ultimately agreed they would embark on the 30 Day Blackout, beginning the next day. They also began preparing themselves for the hell they would pay when they returned home to inform the children.

All of their children had TVs and video games in their bedrooms, which had to be immediately removed. Mom and Dad always assumed everything was fine if their children were occupied and having fun on electronics. The house was peaceful and it gave the parents more quiet time.

But the impact of screens was now crystal clear, and they both knew it. It was time to begin repairing the damage caused by unintentional neglect and too much screen time, and they were now willing to do what was needed to save their family.

The first five days were total hell—lots of yelling, name-calling, slamming doors, bargaining and pointing fingers. There were a few moments of reprieve sprinkled in as they dusted off their board games and put together puzzles, and when they rode their bikes for the first time in years.

By day five, the entire family was still pretty aggravated, primarily at me, which is by design. I have found that it is helpful for the family to have a scapegoat, somebody to be mad at other than mom and dad. You're probably familiar with the old adage: Nothing unites adversaries like a common enemy.

Let me be the enemy. I can take it.

At the beginning of the next session, Maddy's younger brother, Jesse, told his mom he wanted to see me. He came in to tell me he thought the Blackout was working, that all of his siblings had finally come out of their rooms, and they had started putting together a 500-piece puzzle. That was something he had always wanted to do, but the family never seemed to have the time. He wasn't thanking me. He just wanted me to know it was working, which I thought was incredibly insightful for a 7-year-old.

While working with Maddy those first few sessions, I focused on nonverbal, kinesthetic interactions (doing/feeling/sensing) to begin allowing her nervous system to integrate her experiences and come back to a grounded state. We played magnetic darts, tossed a ball, and spent time engaging with small toys in my sand trays—activities that did not require words, nor even much eye contact.

I used a process of parallel play that began allowing her to experience connection in a non-threatening way. By borrowing from my calm, parasympathetic ventral-regulated self, Maddy may enter the beginning stages of the therapeutic experience. When a child can "feel" regulation (a state of grounded calm)

> ### *Parallel Play*
>
> *Children playing next to each other but not with each other. Both building a stack of blocks, but not working on the same tower, for example. Most common from 2 through 5 years of age.*

from a safe, temporary attachment figure, such as a therapist, she can begin to heal. I am there to simply offer her a safe place, without prying or asking any questions.

I usually have classical or peaceful music playing quietly in the background. For a child in a state of hypoarousal (collapse response), I typically turn it up to try and wake up the child's nervous system in an attempt to boost their energy and engagement. I also may take a child for a walk and simply ask, "What can you see? What can you hear? Taste? Touch? Feel?" Although initially reluctant, after feeling a bit of safety with me (through sand trays, art work, and a good game of checkers), the child is willing to at least answer a few of my questions.

With Maddy, I could tell she trusted me, but she didn't trust her parents, which is what I frequently see. Although children want to be like their friends and watch all the latest shows, YouTube videos, video games and the like, at the end of the day those same children will blame their parents for allowing them to see what their young eyes and nervous systems were not ready to experience. This creates an attachment injury that must be repaired.

Several weeks into the process, I choreograph an "I'm sorry" session using my Magic Mats, communication tools where we focus on repairing the attachment bond instead of focusing on the behavior problems of the child.

First, the parents (or parent) take responsibility for allowing the child to be exposed to entirely too much screen time. That usually takes the edge off. Kids are not used to their parents apologizing for something, especially when neither of them thought there was anything really wrong with it.

By the end of the Blackout, I have convinced the family to go camping or hiking, something to get them out of the house and break their normal routine. By this time, they've dusted off their board games and played them so many times they need to experience some new bonding activities.

With Maddy's family, there was a lot of complaining at the beginning. Honestly, with it being football season, I feel pretty certain Dad was cheating on the Blackout. But believe it or not, they saw such fantastic results in their children that the parents decided to repeat the Blackout for another 30 days! This didn't go over well with the children initially, but after the shock wore off and they accepted it, they all started chiming in with activities they hoped to experience together.

> ## Attachment Injury
>
> *An emotional wound to an intimate, interdependent relationship, like that between a parent and child, siblings, partners, spouses, or lovers. Attachment injuries can be caused by severe loss like death, divorce, long absences or major moves. These can also be caused by unresolved anger or resentment, abandonment or the appearance of it, constant conflict, unhealed trauma, lying, betrayal, and fear.*

Maddy continued to get better.

It always makes my heart smile when I see an emotionally shut-down child come back to life. I can always tell because the twinkle in their eyes comes back—they smile without having to work at it. It's a relaxed "I'm a kid" happy, joyous, and free look that we all long for—a gift of childhood—and I would like for all children to keep it as long as they can.

Typically, this look comes back when the nervous system begins to experience a more regulated state. When we start with the Blackout and then focus on the family bond instead of the undesirable behavior, and replace entertainment with connection-based activities, combined with lots of unstructured, nature-based play, we create a scenario where the child can heal. They begin to make eye contact and feel more grounded. The sleep cycles become more stable, and the child is able to communicate what they are feeling and what they need. They not only begin to think more clearly, but they also make more conscious choices while initiating a wide range of emotional expression.

Once we've accomplished this regulated state, I begin working with the siblings in relationship to the child in need, my primary client. The good news is that because the whole family is participating in the Blackout, the siblings' nervous systems have often become regulated as well. During or after the Blackout is when I can observe the sibling relationship for what it is. Many times, there is quite a bit of resentment and misunderstanding in the sibling relationships, and the parents may come to me with concerns about a completely different child in their family.

This is what I humorously call "Whack-a-Mole."

Maybe you've heard of or played the game at an arcade or the county fair where you hit mechanical moles on the head when they pop up from a series of holes. As soon as you hit one, another one pops up. You hit the next one and still another mole pops up. And it goes on and on.

When you start with the original client and get that child's behavior functioning in a healthy way, another one may come along with unhealthy behavior. Don't be discouraged, it happens frequently. If the family chooses to stay the course and climb the entire mountain, this is only part of the process. I have found that disconnection and even perceived trauma through developmentally inappropriate screen time affects the whole family. In my field, the child whose behavior has created the need for mental health services is considered the healthiest member of the family. They are considered the symptom carrier of the dysfunction of the entire family, the one who is smart enough (although subconsciously) to get everybody some help.

Typically, at this point in the treatment process, all of the children's nervous systems have regulated, and yet there is sibling rivalry or general resentment that needs to be addressed. Using my connecting conversation Magic Mats and play sessions, I am able to choreograph interpersonal communication between siblings. In my experience, the sibling rivalry is based on a child's inner belief that there is not enough love to go around. The more a parent bonds with each child, filling up their "love bucket" with a sense of unplugged adventure, the less sibling rivalry there will be at home. Family activities that include everyone, along with proper boundaries and limit setting, are also helpful. I've seen this help families of every variety.

As we near the end of our counseling time, I work briefly on the marriage and parent relationship if the parents are still together, and the co-parent relationship of separated parents, if possible. With couples, I find they are so relieved that their children are okay—thriving, connecting, and happy—they now have the mental space to work on their spousal relationship. I have found that couples that go through the Blackout often experience an increased desire for intimacy, closeness, and companionship. I usually find they are willing to remove the TVs from their bedrooms, which results in more meaningful conversations.

I regularly receive emails and notes from parents thanking me for climbing the mountain with them. If they continue to focus on connection-based activities and togetherness, offering lots of hugs and snuggles, reading books, taking family walks, spending time in nature, and learning to say "no" to too many activities, the families typically do not need to call me back. If they adopt the belief that screen time is like the dessert in their lives, and not the main course, then they can move forward without needing further help from me.

Magic Mats

Even with very difficult cases, the process I've outlined often takes 3-6 months as the family members' nervous systems settle and recalibrate with connection-based activities instead of entertainment. Giving them practical ways to resolve conflicts in everyday life, like with my Magic Mats, helps them to not need ongoing professional help.

I would like to tell you one more story about a little 4-year-old boy named Simon that I walked through the Blackout.

Four-year-old Simon came to my office bright-eyed and bushy-tailed, and not in a good way. He was a cute and feisty young boy, but his parents simply did not know what to do with him. He was hitting and biting his brother, throwing major temper tantrums, not sleeping at night, and he was being very disrespectful toward his parents, teachers, and other children. They were preparing for his first year in kindergarten and knew the trajectory they were on could prove disastrous.

After my traditional play-based assessment, I saw his attention span was maybe 15 seconds at any given time, and his brain was constantly changing lanes without a turn signal. He expected, and even demanded, to be constantly entertained. By the end of the assessment time, not only were the parents exhausted, so was I. This was clearly no way to live. After encouraging the parents to give me an honest assessment, I realized that four-year-old Simon was on screens at least 7-8 hours per day.

I immediately suggested the Blackout, after which the parents looked at me like I had lost my mind and was from some distant planet. I went through my normal explanation, telling them exactly how it works and what they could expect.

By the end of the session, they were reluctant, but willing. I think the dad was the most reluctant, as his leisure time was spent playing video games himself, and he was aghast by what he had just agreed to do.

You see, Simon was an easy patient. Because I had done this so many times before, I knew that if they followed through with the Blackout, they would get their cute, precocious, joy-filled little boy back. He would again be the child they could take to the grocery store and know that he would behave, and it would not be a traumatic experience. I have found that children in a hyperaroused state are typically easier to help regulate than hypoaroused (shut down), so whenever I have a child in my office who is bouncing off the walls, I'm pretty confident that in a few months all will be well if the parents are willing to simply follow the protocol.

And follow the protocol they did. Not perfectly, mind you, but lo and behold a few weeks later little Simon looked at me with his big brown eyes and had a coherent conversation. His parents reported that he was so fun and funny again. They were sad that they had pawned off their child to an electronic, glowing-screen babysitter. They just hadn't known how to parent well at all, and that was difficult to admit. They had used the TV to keep him occupied so they could get their necessary adult activities completed. They really didn't know how to delight in or really "see" their child—but they wanted to learn. They were genuinely apologetic and could hardly believe the difference it had made in just a few weeks.

I'm telling you this to show you the free gift of the nervous system. Our bodies and brains are designed to heal themselves given the right environment. Just like flowers in a garden, given the right soil, water, sun and temperature, they will flourish. Our children were designed to grow naturally. Screens can happily be an add-on to their regulated lives, but they cannot BE their lives.

For 4-year-old Simon, the treatment process, his "climbing the mountain," was simple. First, it required the discipline and regimen of the 30 Day Blackout. Add to that a lot of unstructured, nature-based play, which means a lot of trips to the creek or the local park for short hikes. Engaging in simple connection activities that are disguised as games, those incorporating eye contact like Uno, Go Fish, Checkers, and Tic-Tac-Toe. Time spent swinging in the backyard or playing in rain puddles and mud. Nothing beats playing in the mud when you're four years old! Too messy? That's what garden hoses are for—making mud and rinsing it off.

This particular family continued past the Blackout with what I call a "Grayout" for a second 30 days. That is where the family limits screen time to no more than 30 minutes to an hour of "Slow Screen Time" per day. The Slow Screen Time shows are those such as Mr. Rogers Neighborhood (his entire collection can be found on Amazon Prime), Andy Griffith, I Love Lucy, Thomas the Train, and Little House on the Prairie. These "slow" shows emphasize family and stories. They do not have quick screen changes and are easier for a child's nervous system to process, while supporting pro-social behavior.

Shows and games with quick changes can rev up the nervous system and land you right back to square one. If you go from the Blackout to a Grayout, choose entertainment wisely. You can find a list of recommended shows in the Resources section at the back of the book.

Now you know why screens are harmful. You know that children need nature more than television. That they need eye contact more than video games. You know what this will cost you and that you have more to gain than you'll give up. You know it might be hard, but it will also be worth it.

Are you ready to take the first step up the mountain? Then turn it all off. Everything. The television, the laptop, the desktop, the phones, the tablets, the gaming devices, any gadget with a screen attached to it. Turn them all off and put them away for the next 30 days.

It's time to Blackout.

Slow Action vs. Fast Action

For the sake of simplicity, in this book, television shows and movies are divided into fast and slow action. Slow action looks more like real life. No quick scene or point of view changes, limited special effects, and no flashing lights. The sound is often simple, too. Music is the backdrop, not multiple explosions and people screaming.

Fast action shows are the opposite. Often animated, they feature quick movement, lots of flashing colors and screen changes, and multiple special effects, sometimes to the point that it feels like watching a strobe light. They tend to energize instead of relax.

1. Does your child seem hyperaroused? All revved up? Does it happen at specific times or after specific events (after watching a certain program, eating, waking up, etc.)? Can he/she remain focused for more than a few minutes at a time (or a few seconds)?
2. Do you ever notice a collapse response? This would usually be right after turning off a game or other screen. In extreme cases, your child could be in a collapsed state the majority of the time.
3. Is the majority of what your child sees on screens fast or slow? Live action or animation? If it's a television program, is the focus on relationships and solving problems, or on effects and movement, like an action movie?
4. What do the sibling relationships in your home look like? Be honest. What would you like them to look like?

Interview with Elana

as told to Elizabeth Adams

Elana first came to see Stacy because she had recently gone through a divorce, and her six-year-old daughter had begun having accidents again—wetting her pants at school and at home when she had never had that problem before.

Stacy recommended the Blackout as a way for the family to reconnect.

The first week was difficult, as expected. Elana describes her daughter Charlotte as a master negotiator. She could talk her way out of anything. There was a lot of whining and complaining of boredom. Luckily, Elana and her ex were willing to work together.

"It's one of the few times we have stayed on the same page. We co-parent well. Our daughter is our first priority, our issues fall to the side, and it becomes about how we can be good business partners. We're in the business of raising this child together," says Elana.

At first, it was two steps forward and one step back, but after the first week, Charlotte's natural creativity began to surface. Elana noticed that Charlotte's imagination was more active, and she was more curious than she had been, and more likely to indulge that curiosity.

"The boredom passed faster than I thought it would. She's very artistic," asserts Elana.

She could tell a difference in the quality of Charlotte's play and the way she would interact. Things were shifting.

Because of her daughter's anxiety after the divorce, Elana decided to eliminate sugar at the same time. "Doing both together specifically for my child was the right way. I don't know if we would have gotten the same results if we had just done one. Sugar and screen time can be drugs of choice," says Elana.

Elana's ex occasionally gave in on the sweets, but both parents stuck to the Blackout strictly. Overall, they ended up continuing for 90 days.

Elana had felt guilty for the divorce and that had caused her to let things slide that she normally wouldn't have, like screens and sugar consumption, and she knew she needed to begin to undo the damage.

"I realized this was the most loving thing I could do for her as a parent—to set boundaries, without feeling guilty."

Elana learned not to lean on screens when she needed a minute away. Because Charlotte is an only child, she was used to lots of attention. Not being able to tag off to a screen was hard, but doable. They took the opportunity of the Blackout to start some new family habits and traditions. Elana began working on reattachment—keeping Charlotte with her, having her bring a coloring book or notebook into the room she was working in and sitting together.

They also started a new tradition of Friday night Shabbat dinners. Elana isn't truly Jewish, but she wanted to embrace the tradition. Every Friday night, they have a family dinner and talk about the past week with no phones, no screens, nothing. They talk about what they could have done better or differently and set intentions for the following week, then they play games afterward.

Post-Blackout, Elana's connection to her daughter is stronger. They talk more about feelings, about school, about everything. Communication in general has greatly improved. Now, the family utilizes a marble system (explained in Chapter 5) to regulate screen time and occasionally uses screen time as a reward.

"I don't know that I would have told you how thankful I was in the middle of it, but I absolutely am thankful for it now. It got us where we needed to get."

4

The Talk

When I propose the 30 Day Blackout, I generally recommend a family sit-down discussion that begins with the parent(s) saying something like this:

"Guys, I want to talk to you about something that has been really bothering me for a while now. First, let me say that I'm sad because I realize I was wrong for allowing our family to engage in so much screen time. The truth is, I'm not exactly sure how much time you are on your screens, but I do know that it is way too much. It is taking away from our family time and causing constant chaos and arguing. It is keeping you from reading quality books, from creative projects, from us going and doing things together as a family, and well, I'm just really sad about it. For a while I have noticed there is a problem— but our whole culture seems to be living like this now—so I have minimized it, trying to make it okay. But it's not okay.

"Here is what I know now. We are made to connect—and we are not connecting well. I am taking responsibility for allowing screens to get in the way of us being the family we are supposed to be.

"I met a lady who has been walking families through what she calls a 30 Day Blackout. The Blackout is where we all turn everything off for 30 days—every iPad, tablet, phone, computer, TV, Wii, video games—it all gets turned off for 30 days."

I warn parents to be prepared for moaning, groaning, gnashing of teeth, meltdowns, bargaining,

93

crying, fits of rage, or just plain shock and disbelief. I've had children in my office who had to be scooped up off the floor and carried away when they found out they were losing their screens for 30 days.

The initial news to a child can be devastating—especially if they perceive that their connection needs have been primarily met through screen time. It is a cheap substitute for true connection and allows the child to have their legitimate needs met in an illegitimate way, which is a precursor to addiction of all varieties.

Let me say that again. **We all have needs.** Pretending that we don't is ludicrous. You are not an island and neither is your child. **Need is not weakness.** Love, affection, acceptance, and belonging are basic human requirements. If we do not get those needs met in a legitimate way—from our family and friends—we will attempt to get them met in an illegitimate way. In children, this is often excessive screen time. As they grow older, it becomes food abuse and addiction, eating disorders, porn addiction, drug abuse and addiction, alcohol abuse, dysfunctional relationships, violence and bullying, depression and anxiety.

My intention is not to alarm you, but to impress upon you the gravity of the situation. The nervous system is nothing to fool around with, and emotional security and health are not laughing matters. What happens in our childhoods can stay with us our entire lives. We must think about what we want our children to carry with them into adulthood. Do we want them to take anxiety and a feeling of never belonging, or do we want them to carry confidence and security?

The Blackout seems hard now, but it is nothing compared to watching your child go down the spiral of addiction, watching your child choose an abusive partner, or seeing your child so crippled with anxiety that they can't attend college or hold down a proper job. Right now, you are an active participant in your child's life and have the power to help them. Years down the road, your kids will be independent adults and you'll be an observer.

We have unintentionally (or intentionally in some cases) been passing off our children to a glowing screen babysitter for far too long. An intervention is sometimes the best strategy in order to reclaim and preserve our family life.

What I recommend to lighten the blow is Birdie Talk. Simply empathize with the child by summarizing and repeating back what they are telling you.

"Mom, I wish I could play a game on my tablet."

"Isaac, what I'm hearing you say is you wish you could play a game on your tablet."

You don't have to cave in to what they are requesting. Just let them know you hear them and that you empathize. Then, after the initial discussion, I recommend everyone get outside—go for a walk and let the news sink in.

Talk through the obstacles like, "How will we pull this off with work and school?" Explain that all social and gaming apps will come off the devices (Snapchat, Twitter, Facebook, video games, etc.), and that schoolwork on a tablet or computer will be done in the kitchen or other public room while under close adult supervision. When homework is completed, the device will be put away.

I'm not going to lie to you, many children are so addicted to screens that it feels similar to coming off a controlled substance. Many parents have to lock up their screens in a safe or put them somewhere the child cannot find them. It is hard to believe that it has come to this, but in many cases, it has.

After your walk and initial discussion, I recommend a Family Joint Agreement—a one-page document stating all screens will be turned off for 30 days. If you have a young child that cannot sign their name yet, you can help them sign, or they can simply dip their finger or thumb on an ink pad and their fingerprint can serve as their signature of understanding and commitment. At this point, you have a family agreement with a start and end date, and it's time to prepare.

Many families have plenty of board games, cards, puzzles, and crafts tucked away in closets and drawers that are rarely used. It's time to get those out where children can actually see them, so they can have a visual reminder of what I call the Replacement Principle—for anything taken away, there is a healthy replacement.

> **Replacement Principle**
>
> *When something is taken away, replace it with something else. Take away cookies and replace them with fruit. Take away screens and replace with games and visits to the park. Take away phones and replace with face to face conversations.*

You also need to be prepared for repeating yourself—a lot!

There is a vast spectrum of reactions. For some, it will be a mild inconvenience but not that big of a deal. For others, they will wake up the next day thinking this was all a bad dream. Some feel their whole world is crumbling around them, and they will begin acting out in very unpleasant ways. Remember there will likely be screaming, door-slamming, name-calling and bargaining.

In severe cases of high disconnection in the family and out of control amounts of screen time, hospitalization may be necessary if a child is a danger to him/herself. Not because of the screens per se, but due to the perceived trauma of what they have been exposed to, or what the screens have been covering up—the pain, shame, or story that will bubble up without the screens keeping everything at bay. It's rare for a child to feel suicidal, but it does happen.

96

In those severe cases, the screens have been acting as a distraction, keeping all the pain and agony neatly tucked away. Without the screens, all that nastiness comes oozing out, and in some cases, it can be dangerous. It is rare, but if you have worried about your child in the past or you suspect he may have suicidal thoughts, keep a close eye and call your pediatrician if you're concerned. If it gets really bad, you may need a trip to the emergency room.

In a panic, many families will start doing things I do not recommend, like planning trips to the movie theatre (also a screen), trips to stimulating water parks, Chuck E. Cheese, fast-paced amusement parks, etc. **Please do not do this**. It undermines the process.

The process of boredom is key in the Blackout. We *want* them to be bored—at first. We are trying to make the nervous system regulate—for the sympathetic "rev up" nervous system to get a break and for the parasympathetic, or "calm down" system, to engage. Boredom makes room for connection and creativity.

It is vital to incorporate connecting activities in place of what used to be considered entertainment, utilizing as much unstructured, nature-based and creative play as possible. Every family is different, so here are some ideas: camping, hiking, fishing, walking, picnics, nature walks, crafts, painting, board games, card games, and puzzles are great connecting activities. Reading books aloud, journaling, cooking together, LEGO creations, sewing, knitting... you get the picture.

So for now, I just want you to sit down with your children, have an honest conversation about the Blackout, and get outside to let them process their emotions using Birdie Talk. Focus on the Replacement Principle and plan connection activities for the next 30 days. Then I will walk you through the next step.

Before the talk:

1. Where are you going to have your conversation with the kids? (It should be somewhere private, safe, and comfortable, like at home or in a therapist's office.)
2. Who will do the talking? Who will answer questions? It's important you have this worked out between you and your partner *before* discussing it with the kids.
3. How do you plan to respond to their reactions?
4. What will you do immediately after the talk? Going outside is always a good idea. Back yard? Walk through the neighborhood?

After the talk:

1. How did it go?
2. Were you surprised by anything?
3. Do you have a support system in place for the next few weeks? If not, now would be a good time to call in some back up, even if it's just a quick ten-minute phone call to an old friend.
4. Remember why you're doing this and stay the course. You can do this. And so can they.

Interview with Keisha

as told to Elizabeth Adams

Keisha was in a tough spot. Her eight-year-old daughter Maya was stealing. Anything, anywhere, it didn't matter. She wasn't stealing out of actual need; she wanted for nothing as far as her physical needs were concerned. But she was stealing all over town and Keisha didn't know what to do.

"I was desperate to fix my daughter," says Keisha, "and Stacy said if we did the Blackout it would work faster."

As per usual, one of Stacy's first questions was, "How much screen time?"

Willing to do whatever it would take to help Maya, Keisha agreed to the Blackout. She, Maya, and her five-year-old son Trey were all on board.

Her husband had decided not to participate, but he was respectful of what they were doing and watched television on his own in a room with the door closed and tried not to use screens in front of the kids. Keisha would also watch television when the kids weren't home.

"Day one was a Sunday, which was terrifying because it's a full day without any distractions," says Keisha with a laugh. "It was a rainy season, we could never go out, almost every weekend it poured rain."

That meant lots of board games. They learned how to play Monopoly—two different versions, and the kids never played without Keisha.

"Every game was played with me. They had toys and coloring books that they would go off and do by themselves. And they played together if I wasn't involved."

Thankfully, school took up most of the day on weekdays. Trey, at age five, was only in school until noon. He and Keisha developed a tradition of taking afternoon naps together, something they had not previously indulged in. When Maya came home from school, they would often do a puzzle together.

Maya started to calm down as the Blackout progressed. Prior to the Blackout, Keisha would describe her daughter, "Like a chihuahua. She was just jumping, jumping, jumping. Used to drive me nuts."

Once the Blackout started, it was remarkably easy. "I was taken aback by both of them just accepting the situation. They never complained once. It was unbelievable."

Of course, this might have had something to do with the deal Keisha made with her kids. She sat them down and told them the Blackout was happening and explained exactly what they could expect. Then she took them to the grocery store and allowed them to choose whatever ice cream and toppings they wanted. Their deal? If they could make it through the day successfully with no screens, they could have a small ice cream sundae each night. Keisha figured a little sugar was better than hours on end of screens.

It worked.

Prior to beginning the Blackout, the kids hadn't been big on handheld devices, though they had iPads for the car and restaurants, but those were never allowed in the house. However, inside, the television was almost constantly on.

On weekends they could watch television 24/7 if they wanted. The kids would typically go to sleep with the television on a 30 minute timer. Keisha and her husband didn't pay attention to how slow or fast the action was in a show.

"There was never a rule of what they could or couldn't watch, as long as it was a kids' channel," says Keisha.

When asked what the hardest part of the Blackout was, Keisha had a surprising answer.

"Cutting out the radio in the car. I had no idea how much I depended on distractions in the car. I'm a quiet person, I don't talk a lot to my kids. I probably should talk more," says Keisha. "It took about two weeks to get in a groove; the second two weeks were easier."

That wasn't the only adjustment. Keisha's husband, who had opted not to participate in the Blackout, would occasionally play games with his wife and kids, something the family had never really done before.

"I will say that I feel like my marriage improved overall. We were both so concerned over my daughter. We were the only two who loved her that much, the only two who understood her situation."

Keisha says there was a lot of fighting between her and her husband, and not just over Maya's stealing, but over typical couple stuff as well. "We're very intense people, so it can quickly escalate," she says with a laugh.

Now?

"It's almost night and day."

Having recently completed the Blackout, Keisha's family now watches television within limits, and preferably slower action shows. She also plays board games each weekend with her children.

"I definitely gained a little more insight as to how important it is to spend time with your kids. I didn't grow up like that. I thought my kids would do that too," says Maya. "It's definitely eye opening. I've thought about doing a week or so here or there to reboot."

And the biggest problem they'd been trying to solve?

"From day one all the way through the Blackout, Maya never stole anything. Made me wonder if she just needed attention."

5

What to Expect

If a family is going to hike to base camp together, they need to be fully committed to making it. One way I've found for a family to communicate the seriousness and adventure of the Blackout is to start by discussing two things.

Where are we now at the beginning of this hike?

What do we want to achieve at the end?

Another way to frame the question is, "If someone had a magic wand and could transform our family, what would it look like?"

The first step to climbing the mountain is a full commitment to the Blackout. As mentioned in Chapter 4, I recommend a Family Joint Agreement—a one-page document stating that everyone in the family agrees to turn off all electronic devices for 30 days. If limited screen time is allowed, the agreement should outline specific guidelines and limits around it.

For example, if you have teenagers and younger children, the older children could be allowed 30 minutes of time each evening to connect with their peers via FaceTime or texting, avoiding Snapchat and social media, then they have to turn in their phones to you before going to bed. In cases such as these, it is imperative that the older children are not using their devices in front of the younger, but rather after the younger children are in bed or otherwise occupied. And the potential limited screen time cannot interfere with family time in any way.

I see parents in my office who truly want their child back, and they understand the critical importance of helping a child's nervous system regulate. But for a variety of reasons (divorce being the most common), both parents simply cannot get on the same page.

This is when I recommend a 30 Day Grayout. A Grayout is when a family decides that, for reasons beyond their control, a 30 Day Blackout is just not possible. This Grayout is a compromise to limit screen time to no more than 30 minutes to one hour per day. Preferably, this limited time on screens should be slow action shows like *Mr. Rogers Neighborhood, Sesame Street, I Love Lucy, Andy Griffith, Max and Ruby,* or *Thomas the Train.* Or, as a last resort, the sports channel for those who just can't stomach the idea of missing a game. Preferably, commercials and advertisements are skipped because when the hour is over, it's over.

This is an acceptable compromise when one parent wants to go ahead with the Blackout and the other parent doesn't. The same Family Joint Agreement applies and the guidelines, as well as any modifications (*do this at Parent A's house and this at Parent B's house*), are stated clearly. Everyone's signature affirms their commitment to reducing technology as much as possible for 30 days in order to help reset the child's brain, regulate his nervous system, and get to the root of any behavioral or connecting problems at home.

Once the Family Joint Agreement is signed, it's time to begin the Blackout.

Week 1

It's About to Go Down

Week One is total hell. If your child was out of control before the Blackout, go ahead and prepare yourself for it to be worse as the Blackout begins. Most families I work with do not know what to do with a child whose behavior or nervous system is dysregulated, and their strategy, their default, is to just give them more dysregulating, high-energy screen time. This is the equivalent of giving a child more and more candy and expecting them to remain calm and never develop a stomachache.

It just doesn't work.

What I have found is that over the first five days some children become hyperaroused, which means lots of acting out. This may manifest itself as name-calling, door-slamming, fit-throwing, and other disruptive acts.

In some cases, the child may become hypoaroused, which is when a child acts listless, reclusive, or depressed. They will not engage with you and seem to be living in some far-off place.

Here's what I recommend parents do in the first five days.

Most importantly, get the child outside. Let them feel the sun on their face and the wind in their hair. Have them bend down and touch the grass. Take them for a hike, a walk, a bike ride—anything with bilateral stimulation, which is a steady left-right, left-right movement (think cycling, swimming, walking, etc.). This is helpful in bringing a child who has been isolated and on too many screens back to the land of the living.

Another important activity during the first five days is to break out your board games. Some children are immediately grateful for the time and attention, but most

105

will fuss and push back. Board games and cards aren't as exciting as the video games they've been playing, and it can feel like moving to a campground after having lived in an urban high-rise all your life.

Don't expect anything productive to occur for the first five days—it's like cutting coffee out of your diet. The first few days are the longest and most difficult.

Expect a lot of negotiating. A lot! The child may even want to call me to tell me what a bad idea this is. Don't be discouraged. Stay the course. Many children have never known life without screens, so it may be a very odd and seemingly unfair experience at first. This can produce some unexpected reactions and kids can get quite creative in an attempt to get what they want.

One of the most impressive examples of this was a boy named Ivan. Ivan was a bright, competitive boy of eight. His parents came to me looking for help with his younger sister's behavior and, as a result, the entire family ended up doing the Blackout together. Remember, in family therapy, the one receiving treatment is the symptom carrier—the flare sent up from a stranded boat, the white flag flown in a battle.[15] Based on everything I had seen with his sister and parents, I knew the family as a whole had some dysfunction to work through. Ivan came to me at the beginning of his sister's next session and proceeded to tell me, with impressive clarity, that I had made a terrible mistake. He did not need a Blackout. He needed to play games with his friends. He was on a team, and they were counting on him. Did I not understand that?

He made his case strongly, but I could tell by the anxious way he was bouncing and tapping his fingers, not to mention that for all his ability to speak convincingly, he could only look at my face for a few seconds before scanning the room, that his nervous system was dysregulated, just not to the same extent as his younger sister's.

106

I smiled at Ivan and told him that I saw he was frustrated and that I knew this was hard, but that it would get easier soon. In the meantime, he could try playing different kinds of games with his parents and siblings or with any friends who came over. You can imagine his reaction. Eyes rolled. Shoulders rose in frustration and sank back down in resignation. Hands balled into angry fists.

My heart went out to him, truly, but I knew what his parents were doing was for the ultimate best, for him and his family as a whole. Usually these confrontations are humorous and leave me admiring the tenacity of a child willing to confront an adult over an issue they believe is important. It gives me hope that the same tenacity will be put toward greater goals once his system is regulated and his mind is free to think about more than the next game level or the latest episode of his favorite show.

This reaction is not uncommon or unexpected. All these children have ever known is the frantic activity on their screens. So, for many children, the Blackout is like a trust fall—they are falling back, hoping for a safe, loving person that is bigger and stronger than they are who will catch them in a gentle way. They are too young to articulate this and probably don't even know what it is they are feeling, so I articulate it for them by simply saying this: "I know you're scared. And I promise you're going to be all right. It's okay to be mad at me." And then I give them a hug. Nothing has changed with regard to the Blackout, and they leave my office feeling a bit perplexed, but soothed by the knowledge that **someone is in charge, and finally it's not them.**

Children know they are children. They realize they cannot drive a car, prepare a meal, or buy anything at the store. They can't even arrive late to school without a note. They understand this world is not run by them and that they are surrounded by people bigger and stronger than they are. They may not say this, but they feel it. They feel their own smallness in a big world.

Do you really think I should be calling the shots here?

So they look to you. To their parents, grandparents, aunts and uncles, teachers, neighbors, babysitters. If these people allow the child to do whatever he or she wants, the child then feels that he is in charge. And that is a terrifying prospect.

Whether it looks like it or not, kids like boundaries. They like knowing what they can and cannot do and what they can and cannot expect from the adults in their lives. Note: **Boundaries and control are not the same thing.** Setting limits for your child is not the same as controlling them. Many adults had controlling parents and have compensated for this by allowing their children free rein. This usually results in rude, unruly, difficult children raised by well-meaning parents. Be careful not to fall into this trap.

If you have more than one child, you know each one is different. One may be more spontaneous than the other. One may like more structure while the other likes more freedom. That's normal and nothing to worry about. But one thing all children need is security on a basic level. They need an adult in the room who knows how to handle simple things like locks and windows, but more importantly, who knows how to handle *them*, and to do so with care.

Most children do not learn how to manage their emotions until well into adolescence and beyond. Some people have never learned. That's why when an adult is petulant or whiny we say he is acting like a child. A child feels things in a big way. They can be frightened by their own emotions and reactions. Much of life is still new to them and therefore scary. They need adults in their lives who can guide them and give them a secure anchor to which they can tether themselves.

This is why I tell them it's okay to be mad at me. It's why I tell them exactly what's going to happen and why the parents tell them, too. It's why there is a contract delineating details and the timeline of the Blackout. They know what's coming and on some level, what to expect. They need that assurance from me and from you that it will all be all right, because **for a child's tiny world, this can be a big change.**

Kids aren't the only ones who feel intimidated at the idea of the Blackout. Multiple parents over the years have sent me emails and messages during the first five days saying, "Are you sure this is going to work? Why do we have to do this, too? Are you sure we need to do this for 30 days? Why not just a week?"

Because Rome wasn't built in a day. You didn't get here in a week, and you won't get out in a week, either. Show your children you're strong. Show them they can rely on you. The world is a scary place, but that's why we have parents.

The truth is, turning off screens for a time requires you to connect back to yourself. You are no longer trying to get your connection needs met via screens, and the person you spend most of your time with is yourself. Turning off screens alienates you from the electronic world and allows, and actually requires, time for quiet reflection.

If you are spending time in an unstructured nature-based activity, with bare feet on the soil or grass, you are reconnecting to yourself and to nature, something many of us have forgotten about in these modern times. When you spend time in nature, it helps to regulate your nervous system—you become more ventrally activated, the part of your parasympathetic nervous system that allows you to feel a sense of being grounded, mindful, and connected to self and others—and a sense of peace comes over you.

You begin to live life in real time, moment by moment, appreciating the nuances of life and health and relationships. You stop taking things for granted. You become mindful of the moment—the smell of your coffee, the laughter in your child's eyes, the grass under your feet. You become aware of the people around you, the interactions of kindness, the opportunities for small acts of connection, and love, and being.

True life is lived in relationship, and it requires a sense of awareness that is difficult to maintain when it's constantly hijacked by screens. But when screens become the dessert of your life rather than the main course, you will find that screens become an added bonus to a full and meaningful life, rather than life itself.

I liken screen time in this day and age to when cigarette advertising was widely prevalent in the 1970s and 80s. There were marquees everywhere—the Marlboro Man, Virginia Slims—featuring elegant photos of men and women smoking as if a cigarette in your hand was a sign of success.

Years later society saw the horrific results of that behavior in the form of diseased lungs and premature death. We are all now keenly aware of the dire consequences of lighting the match and making the choice to smoke.

We don't yet have enough data to know the long-term effects of screens on our brains, nervous systems, and relationships. But if we are smart, we'll use our knowledge of history and the research on the importance of connection and attachment to recognize that a simple intervention like the 30 Day Blackout can return us to what we know works. Eye contact works. Simple things like conversations around the dinner table and cooking together work. Walks in nature work.

It's time to get back to basics.

Days six and seven of the Blackout are transition days. Be prepared for boredom to set in. The nervous system may go through a dorsal parasympathetic collapse, which is when part of your nervous system goes into a constricted state. Feeling withdrawn is common.

These two days are great for reading together as a family, going on family hikes, beginning a family project like a 500-piece puzzle that may take the rest of the Blackout period to complete, or sampling a collection of recipes you've put off trying for months. I refer to these as the "Are You Kidding Me?" days. These are the days the kids will be negotiating with you and telling you what a terrible idea this is. The days they cannot for the life of them find something productive to do. They might mope, cry, have angry outbursts or say things they don't really mean.

Here is what I suggest. If you had a grandmother you were fond of, think about what she would do back in your childhood days. Grandma would break out her crocheting or bake a homemade pie. She would take everybody on a trip to the local farmers market, or lake, or children's museum, or pool. Or she might just take you out in the backyard to the swing. Focus on anything that creates a feeling of mindfulness.

What is mindfulness?

Mindfulness is the mental state of being aware of the present moment, while calmly acknowledging and accepting one's feelings, thoughts, and bodily sensations. This is a wonderful therapeutic technique. Practically speaking, it is teaching yourself and your child how to slow down and be in the present. Not tomorrow. Not yesterday. Right here, right now.

Depression is about the past—being down about what happened yesterday. Anxiety is about the future—trying to figure out what might happen tomorrow. Mindfulness is about the present—being okay with what is happening right now. There is a mindfulness exercise after Chapter 7 to practice connecting with your senses and surroundings if you want to try it.

Week 2

Hello, Drama

There is typically a newfound willingness in Week Two because the child's nervous system has had an opportunity to relax after seven days without revving up the sympathetic nervous system with a variety of screens.

As this happens, the child is less likely to ask for or expect to experience shocking, developmentally inappropriate, or overstimulating content over and over again. Prior to the Blackout, that type of content had kept him in a constant state of unnecessary stress that exacerbates behavioral problems. The parasympathetic dorsal collapse response (that withdrawn, numbed out experience) has hopefully subsided and the child's parasympathetic ventral branch of his nervous system is becoming engaged. This is when a child becomes willing to do things he was not willing to do before, like chop vegetables with dad in the kitchen, go for simple family walks, and play engaging board games with his siblings. The child may begin to find a newfound sense of creativity, such as coming up with art projects, storytelling, creative writing, or creating new structures with piles of blocks or Legos.

This is a time when you listen to your child and try to get to know her personality. What does she like? What does she like to do? How does she best receive affection and love? Does she like to snuggle? Does she want you to play with her? Pay attention and get to know your child as if you were studying a subject in school.

This is also a time to examine your own screen time use. Is it difficult to put down your phone unless it is absolutely necessary? Can you leave it in the car overnight or is it calling your name? Can you find things to do to replace your own screen time, like read a book, try a new recipe, or have coffee with a neighbor?

How about volunteering somewhere to get a new perspective on life? So much of life is about perspective, and I have found the 30 Day Blackout to be extremely helpful in allowing families the freedom to experience life in the here-and-now. I have seen families take their children on hikes for the first time, sing and play instruments, go to church or synagogue, or simply sit in silence and enjoy it.

Week two can also feel like a start and stop in terms of progress. Children who have not experienced their own feelings very many times have a difficult time regulating their emotions during this time period. If they have been consuming a lot of television, internet, and video games, especially those that have a character they are "being," their emotions have been coming from the content of whatever they have been viewing. If it was violent, they may have felt fear and most likely the rush of adrenaline. Racing games can cause a burst of frantic excitement. Often, whatever the character in the game or show is feeling, your child is feeling, too. Children will have different levels of sensitivity and identification with characters. The Blackout can help you and your child realize your own level of sensitivity and establish boundaries accordingly.

Turning everything off and allowing the quiet to come in will allow whatever is going on with your child to bubble to the surface. They feel overwhelmed because they are feeling their own authentic emotions—for the first time in some cases—and have never learned how to deal with them. An emotionally intelligent person can tell you what they feel, what they need and ask to have a need met. A person or child without this intelligence will simply feel overwhelmed and lost, without understanding what they should do to relieve their pain.

This is where parents and caregivers come in. Be calm, be kind, be comforting. Lots of hugs and patience will likely be necessary. You may even notice this happening to some degree with yourself. If you have been getting your need for contact met through social media, or your validation through likes and comments on various posts, you may feel bereft of community when those things suddenly go away. You may feel lonely or realize that you've *been* feeling lonely for a while now, but have been too busy to notice.

Turn to your friends. Turn to your partner. Lean on each other. If desired, turn to a therapist or a faith leader. Cuddling with a pet can also be very soothing.

If you have no partner and your cat isn't very affectionate, or you are not active in a faith community or simply don't have anyone in your life who thinks this is a good idea, you're not alone.

Lisa was a single mom with three children under twelve. Needless to say, the Blackout was hard to do on her own with kids old enough—and tenacious enough—to argue about it incessantly with her. Between the long hours at work, the second shift of house duties when she got home, and trying to be a good mom, she was tired and stressed. Her ex-husband lived a few hours away and only saw the kids once a month. She had no family nearby. There was no one to tag off to. She had been holding it all together by herself for so long that I could see the exhaustion etched into her features.

The kids' father had given them all tablets for Christmas the year before, and it felt like the only time she got a break from the relentless requests and parental responsibilities was when they were playing games or chatting with their friends online. Taking the screens away was a lot more than just removing electronics in an effort to help her kids. It meant giving up her own down time and creating a lot more work for herself.

115

It was a daunting task, but Lisa knew she had to do something. Her youngest, Cora, was so hyper Lisa thought she might actually begin to bounce off the walls. The only time Cora would sit still was while watching a show. It's easy to see why Lisa let her watch—the programs were in line with her morals and values, and some of them were even the slow action shows that other professionals and I recommend. But Cora was a sensitive child and only seven years old. The combination of her personality and her young age meant that she could handle less screen time than her brothers.

Lisa's boys, Jason and Nate, were 12 and nine. Jason had friends at school, but she was beginning to see some disturbing behavior. He was occasionally aggressive, a relatively new behavior for him, and he was increasingly disrespectful to his mother. Lisa knew it was more than just adolescence creeping in. Jason snapped at her most often when she interrupted his time on his phone—he didn't react that way if she spoke to him while he was doing homework. She never saw his face anymore. He was always looking down, staring at a screen, talking to his friends—his entire world lived in a three by five glowing rectangle.

Her middle son was the opposite. Often thought of as her easiest child, Nate was sweet and helpful. And entirely too quiet. As the years went by, especially after his parents' divorce, he became more and more withdrawn. He often failed to respond to basic requests or greetings and spent more and more time in his room on his own—with his tablet.

Lisa was worried about her kids, and for good reason. She was concerned for herself. She was all alone and struggling as it was. How was she going to handle the inevitable outbursts the Blackout would cause?

I'll tell you what I told Lisa: **build a support system**! Get people at work to do the Blackout with you. They don't have to be close friends, just someone you could share the experience with, commiserate with when it's rough, and rejoice with when you see breakthroughs. Talk to neighbors, people at church, other parents at school. Read this book for book club and have everyone do the Blackout together. Whatever you can do to build support will help you—especially if you don't have a partner in the trenches with you.

For situations like Lisa's, I'm going to recommend something a little counterintuitive. Lisa was not addicted to screens. Lisa was not on her phone all day. She looked at a computer at work, but when she got home, she wanted a glass of wine and a bubble bath, not another glowing screen that made her eyes hurt. She would check in with her Facebook account occasionally, but she was far from glued to a screen. For Lisa, social media was what is should be: support when she needed it and a way to connect and keep up with friends and family living far away.

In her case, hopping online a few times a week—alone in her room after the kids had gone to bed—to get support for the Blackout worked. She set a timer so she wasn't on too long, and she was able to connect with a group of other parents who were doing the same thing. It uplifted her and gave her the push she needed to get through the hard days. She did not click on videos of dogs surfing or cats playing with their own reflections. She got on for the purpose of doing one thing, and she stuck to that one thing.

If you think you can do that and you are otherwise alone, joining an online group for support may be for you. If you already spend a lot of time on screens, or if when you go online, you find yourself doing all sorts of things you hadn't intended to do and hours go by without you realizing it, then an online support group is not a good idea for you. Reach out to a friend or family member instead. Even if they live hundreds of miles away, ask if you can set up a phone call once or twice a week to chat about what you're doing with your family. Sometimes a friendly ear gives you the strength you need to keep going.

Conflict Rising

Sibling rivalry may be at an all-time high during this week because learning to share has not been a priority, or practiced much, until now. Using words of kindness may not have been modeled well, so you may hear your children being unkind to one another. Expect name calling and plenty of arguments over things like toys and pets.

This is a time to practice radical acceptance. This too shall pass. Make a "Blackout Box"—a simple shoe box covered in black construction paper. When you notice something good that is coming from the Blackout, write it on a sheet of paper and put it in your Blackout Box to remind yourself at the end of the day of the positives the family is experiencing throughout this process. The box may seem empty sometimes, but I promise, it will start to fill up.

Another challenge some families realize during Week Two is that one partner might not be as willing as the other to engage in the Blackout. If you find yourself in this situation, I recommend using the following conversation starters to address the issue:

> I feel _____.
> I need _____.
> Would you be willing to _____?

For example, you might say, "I feel sad we have not been connecting well as a family. I need this 30 Day Blackout to be as effective as it can be for all of us. Would you be willing to participate as fully as you possibly can in this?"

If your partner refuses to turn off screens at all, ask them to respect what you are trying to do and use screens quietly and behind closed doors, or out of the home if possible. Watch shows and games at a friend's home or sports bar, etc.

If your partner is resistant, it is okay. Just do the best you can. I have found that even if a family cannot fully Blackout, they can still see benefits by dramatically reducing screen time, and change begins to happen.

Week 3

Creativity Unleashed

During the third and fourth weeks, families typically begin to reap the benefits of their decision to participate in the Blackout.

One participation activity my family loves is called Rose/Bud/Thorn. The Rose is something that has made them feel happy or joyful that day. The Bud is something they are hoping for. The Thorn is something that is difficult or something that is making them feel sad. We go around the table at our house and each person shares. Some family members may have a difficult time not interrupting each other or taking turns. If patiently waiting their turn is not something your kids can do, then get an artificial rose and whoever is holding the rose is the one talking, while everyone else gets to listen and wait their turn.

I encourage many of the families I work with to take a camping trip in Week Three or Four. I realize this is dependent on the weather and schedules but try to make it work if you can. I have found that children who have been exposed to too much screen time need a prolonged experience in nature during these two weeks. If it is winter and camping outdoors is not an option, consider renting a cabin at a state or national park. They generally have low rates. If budget and time allows, you could consider getting away somewhere warm for a few days and taking daily nature walks or visiting the beach. The ocean is wonderfully restorative. Best of all, you can enjoy all these places have to offer without needing a phone or device of any kind.

There is a self-healing element to nature that cannot be replaced with a screen, no matter how hard we try. By slowing down, children who have a few days in the woods many times come back with what I call "the twinkle." At the beginning of the Blackout, most children's twinkle in the eye is long gone—that innocent wonder that is a true gift of childhood has been lost somewhere in virtual space, driven away by modern hectic schedules.

Many times, after a long weekend in nature, a child will come back with a newfound hope for relationship and connection. Going on hikes, taking naps in hammocks, making simple meals outside, swinging— all these foster a stronger connection to self. This hope may be something they have never experienced before, or haven't in a long while, and that brings about a peace and contentment only found in what I call the "I am Here" moment—the right here, right now.

The biggest change most parents notice is how creative their children suddenly become. Many children find a newfound interest in drawing, painting, making music, writing stories, and playing inventive games. Creativity is something that each of us is born with, but as we age and conform to society's expectations, we lose that urge to make something beautiful and interesting.

Creativity can take many forms outside the obvious paint on canvas. It can be a daring block tower or a model airplane painstakingly put together. It's solving the unsolvable problem or restoring an old bicycle. It wears many hats and speaks every language.

It's the life force that beats in all of us. Without it, we feel listless and unfulfilled. We yearn for something, but don't always know what it is. Creativity is the song we were born to sing.

It's fingers in the paint. It's the day-long chalk drawing you jump in and find yourself in a world of imagination. Creativity is the doodle drawing you pour into, just to find a new piece of paper to doodle away again. Creativity is the conversation had in a slow rocking chair on the porch with a friend, taking the time to share your thoughts, dreams, and plans with one that has the time to listen and cry and wonder with you.

It's hands in dark, muddy soil, digging for worms. It's mud pies and caterpillars. Butterflies and fountains. Fields of flowers and wide blue skies. Skipping and soaring, jumping and kite flying.

True, unadulterated creativity is the underlying gift of the Blackout, and one of the biggest reasons I started it. It is a ticket to freedom and a key to the heart. The juice that makes us feel alive, free, mindful, soaring, proud, content, and present in joy. The 30 Day Blackout gives us permission to wonder. It makes space for creativity to thrive in our lives.

Week 4

Deep Breath Now

Now let's be real. Many children in Week Four go straight into a countdown to when they will get their screens back. There can be an underlying anxiety that many children cannot verbalize as they subconsciously realize they have been dependent on screens for some time to 1) entertain them, 2) give them a feeling of connection, and 3) fit in with friends. And there are certainly wonderful benefits to the computerized age, but not at the expense of a child experiencing the natural world.

In Week Four I recommend a family discussion where the parents honestly assess their child's behavior. Are they seeing marked improvement? Is the child connecting well? Does it seem like the child is able to regulate his emotions? Is she making eye contact? Being kind? Able to bounce back from setbacks?

If the answer is yes, congratulations, you've done great work. But the work is not complete. It is very important that you do the following during this time period:

1) Put parental controls on all devices. I recommend Net Nanny, the Disney Circle App, and the Screen Time App. It is imperative that children navigate the internet safely.

2) Decide how you are going to be intentional about not allowing any more than an hour per day of leisure-based screen time for your children once the Blackout is completed (either with the screen time marble system or the Screen Time App system). I recommend as much of the allotted screen time to be as slow as possible. If your child is more energized after watching something,

or seems hyper or manic, that show was too fast-paced and/or they watched it too long.

I have found that families who follow the screen time marble system as a token economy for pro-social/good behavior are the biggest winners in the battle for screen time balance.

What is the screen time marble system? At the beginning of the week, once the Blackout is over, of course, each child gets a jar with seven marbles in it. Each marble equals 30 minutes to one hour of screen time, to be decided by the parents, and generally only one marble can be used per day. The marbles can be cashed in a little each day or a few at a time, such as for a big movie night on the weekend. Parents have their own stash of marbles and can add a marble to the child's jar for good behavior, or they can take one away if a behavioral problem arises.

After a while, the family typically gets in the habit of a new screen time routine that is balanced and healthy with proper limits in place. I typically recommend using the marble system for four to six months before retiring them. You can stop using them when you've found a new normal that is stable and reliable.

If your child has not made the amount of progress you were hoping for or what is needed by Week Four, I would ask you to do the Blackout again. Many of my clients who have seen great improvement in their children during the 30 days are unsure what will happen when the screens get turned back on. They feel that reintroducing screens might be a bit premature. If something good is happening and turning the screens back on might prevent that full

> **Pro-Social Behavior**
>
> *Behavior designed to benefit and cooperate with those around us. Compassion. Sympathy. Kindness. Generosity. The opposite of anti-social.*

benefit, they simply let the children know that for X and Y reasons, we will be blacking out for another 30 days.

For children who have been holding their breath waiting to get their screens back, doing another Blackout will frequently cause a stir—an "it's not fair" response that may not be pretty. This is an opportunity for deeper healing in your family. An opportunity to grieve the family connection time you have lost to screens, a time to truly look at each other in the eyes and say, "I'm sorry."

Think about what you would like to accomplish together in these next 30 days. You should draw another mountain together and talk about what you would all want when you reach the top. Have a connecting family conversation about what the top looks like to you and share openly and honestly with one another.

If you choose a second Blackout, this is typically a time for tremendous healing and growth. It is in the quiet spaces that we hear each other more clearly, that we see where we are in our lives with more transparency, and we become more honest in our journey.

You may find at this juncture that you would benefit from seeing a professional child and family therapist to help you with your blind spots. I highly recommend finding a registered play therapist with expertise in trauma and attachment. Visit a4pt.org for a list of registered play therapists in your area.

Whether you choose one Blackout or two, what you are looking for above all else is a relaxed and centered nervous system in your child. You don't have to get overly scientific about this. Just know that the more a child feels safe, secure, seen, heard, celebrated, and delighted in with lots of unstructured nature-based play, the more likely his ventral parasympathetic state will be open and relaxed. This allows for easier connections, which helps reduce behavior problems and becomes his new normal.

The combination of the Blackout, unstructured nature-based play, connection-based activities, and an approachable solution to conflict management within the family is a prescription for contentment, joy, and greater happiness.

Week One:
1. Get ready. It's about to get hard. Do you have a support system in place? Do you need to join the online support group? Is that something you can realistically handle? Can you set up a weekly call with a loved one?
2. What's happening? Is it as bad as you expected? Worse? Better?
3. Make your Blackout Box and start filling it up.

Week Two:

1. How is it going? Are you getting support?
2. What are you noticing with your kids?
3. What are you noticing with yourself?

Week Three:

1. Is it getting any easier? Have you found a groove?
2. Has your family developed any new habits or traditions?
3. Keep in contact with your support team. It's not over yet.
4. Are you noticing increased creativity in your kids or in yourself?

Week Four:

1. Hopefully you're finding a new normal now. Have any relationships in the house changed? Between siblings? Between you and your partner? Parents and children?
2. Has anyone else noticed a change? Teachers, friends, babysitters?

3. Do you feel like you are where you want to be or almost there?
4. Does it feel like anyone is holding their breath, waiting for the Blackout to end?
5. Have you installed parental controls on ALL screens, including your own phone? If you haven't, now's the time.

Interview with Alice

as told to Elizabeth Adams

Alice mostly decided to do the Blackout for her younger son. She has two boys, four and seven, and the youngest was getting a little out of control.

Their household had recently experienced some major changes. They moved from Virginia to Tennessee, and Dad had gone ahead while Alice stayed behind with the boys so her oldest, Ethan, could finish the semester. The family was separated for three months, and it took its toll.

Once the family was reunited, David, then four, began to show all the fear and upset he had been feeling for the last several months. He became extremely disobedient to the point that he wouldn't get dressed or leave the house with the family.

Because they were new to the area, they stayed with Alice's parents while looking for a place to live. That's when they started seeing Stacy. She, of course, recommended they reduce their screen time. Alice and her husband John tried to cut back, but it wasn't enough and didn't make much of a difference.

"You should have seen Stacy's face when we told her they were watching TV six to eight hours a day," says Alice.

The kids didn't have their own phones or tablets, but the TV came on in the morning when everyone got up and was turned off when they left for school. As soon as the kids got home, they turned it back on and it stayed on until bedtime. It wasn't just background noise. They were paying attention to the programs the majority of the time.

Eventually, they realized doing things halfway wasn't going to work. They agreed to do the full 30 Day Blackout, but Alice still wasn't entirely convinced.

"I thought it was bull, honestly."

She decided to start when her parents left town for a vacation. Given how much time they had spent watching television, it's no surprise that the children were not happy with the idea of blacking out.

They argued. They cried. They bargained and tried to convince their parents it was stupid and unnecessary. There was a lot of anger and a lot of pushback, but John and Alice held firm. Alice says she was thinking in the back of her mind that if it didn't work out, they could just turn everything back on.

The first week was hell on wheels. Ethan, then seven, was sure Stacy had made a terrible mistake. He told his mother that he wanted to talk to Miss Stacy, certain he could convince his therapist to take back her horrible instructions and give him his TV back. Alice told him to go ahead. Of course, Stacy said no.

The difficulty and drama lasted about a week, then Alice's parents came home from vacation. They immediately noticed a difference. When Alice asked her mother what kind of difference, she said the boys were much calmer.

Alice was shocked. For her, the week had been anything but calm.

"When you're in the trenches, you don't know if you're winning or losing. You just keep fighting," says Alice.

Clearly, they were winning the battle. After the first week, she began to notice changes, too. The boys were less intense with each other. They wrestled and fought less and were able to focus on what the other was saying as well as on what their parents were saying. They were more relaxed when on their own and with others.

"I asked Ethan's teacher if she saw any change and she immediately said yes. He was paying attention more and much calmer."

The recognition continued to roll in: from teachers, church members, and friends. The boys were kinder, more present, less manic.

The Blackout was working.

Screen time wasn't the only thing that changed. John and Alice changed their parenting style, too.

"It changed everything we knew about parenting. Not that we were doing it wrong, but we weren't doing what they needed."

Alice and her husband had both been easy-going, compliant children. Ethan and David were anything but. John and Alice were parenting for the children they had been, not the children they have. And they were learning that even though both their boys were non-compliant, they couldn't necessarily be parented the same.

Ethan was in first grade, so he spent the day in school, but David—the original client—was only four years old and attended a parent's-day-out twice a week. That meant Alice was on her own with a small child for most of the day. Without TV or the distraction of her phone, she was running short on ideas.

"The hardest part was filling the time. We did a puzzle, he's done, I'm done. Now what?"

They window shopped. They went to the post office to collect the mail. They strolled through furniture stores, home improvement stores—anywhere that didn't have a toy department.

Somehow, they muddled through and made it to the end of their 30 days.

Stacy's therapy practice follows a designed course, and when the family reaches their goals, they graduate. Alice and her family got where they wanted to be, and they happily graduated.

Then they started letting screens back in, bit by bit.

Six weeks later, they were back in family therapy.

"It's a slippery slope. It's so easy to fall back into old habits," says Alice.

Her youngest is particularly susceptible to screens. After an hour, hour and a half, it gets bad.

"If we let him watch TV on Saturday morning, we pay for it later."

So they did something radical. They made the Blackout a lifestyle. Alice isn't the type to keep up with something like the marble system, so she takes a more cut and dry approach. Absolutely no screens unless it's a little *Mr. Rogers* on the weekends or family movie night. The boys are allowed to play video games on Sunday afternoons if they are good.

That's it.

Alice and John had always tried to live a non-busy life. They weren't super involved in extracurricular activities, not a lot of sports or after school clubs. They wanted a calm and quiet lifestyle, but they hadn't fully achieved it yet.

"The calm we were looking for came in when the TV went off," says Alice.

And the kids calming down wasn't the only improvement. John and Alice grew closer, too. They became more intentional about spending time together. They don't live a full Blackout lifestyle themselves, but have drastically reduced their screen time overall.

"When the TV is on, you're watching, not connecting. If we don't connect before we turn the TV on at night, we are not going to connect that day. It's disrupting to our connecting time."

When it comes to living the Blackout as a lifestyle, it's a delicate path to tread. Two years in, Alice worries her sons will miss out on some elements of popular culture or appear weird or odd to their peers. At the same time, she knows it's what is best for her family. It's a delicate dance, and as the boys grow, they adjust and shift as they need to, but the results have been worth it. There are no longer fights to get out the door, or go to bed, or to get dressed. The boys don't fight with each other as often, and they read significantly more, something Alice never thought would happen.

Ethan has even begun writing his own stories with his free time.

"I try to tell others about it. I try to evangelize," says Alice. Like with her sister-in-law, whose son watches a lot of television and his mom thinks he has ADHD because he can't focus. "Maybe if he watched less television…"

While Alice shares with those whom she thinks need it, she doesn't go overboard. "People look at you like you're weird. I try not to tell too many people because I don't want to start anything, or sound holier-than-thou."

However, after two years of living a Blackout lifestyle, she does have one piece of sage advice. "I tell parents with young kids not to start with TV, because if you don't start, you won't have to do a Blackout. Because it's the worst thing," she laughs. "It's hard!"

134

6

What Now?

You've turned off the TV, taken away the tablets and phones, unplugged the game consoles, and reduced or eliminated computer use. Maybe your kids are instantly thrilled with the changes and spend all their free time making watercolors and knitting scarves for their grandparents.

Maybe not.

If you have a child at home all day, school children in the afternoons and weekends, or if you're on summer break, you're probably wondering what you're going to do with all that spare time now that you can't fall back on movies and video games.

If you're not the Mary Poppins type, brimming over with unique and magical ideas, this might be a little daunting. Having some ideas in your back pocket can help you get through the Blackout, especially the first couple of weeks when you're getting the hang of it. You've just gotten a lot of information and you might be feeling a little overwhelmed. It's important to keep moving forward and not to become paralyzed with the weight of everything that's happening. This chapter is designed to do just that: keep you moving forward.

Something to keep in mind: if I take some time first thing in the morning to give my kids my undivided attention—snuggling with a book, coloring a picture together, having a chat over a cup of tea—they are then ready to face the day with all the security of knowing they are well loved and cared for. They interrupt less, complain less, and allow me to get done what I need to do. In talking to other moms, I realized they've noticed the same thing, too. This may not be possible for you on a daily basis, but give it a try on a weekend.

Hopefully, the Blackout will give you a chance to get in touch with your own creativity and ideas will come to you more rapidly. But for right now, here are some tips to get going.

Back to the Table

There's a reason business deals are often arranged at dinner. Why clients get taken out for drinks and wined and dined on the company dime. Why marriage proposals happen during a romantic meal. Why religious gatherings often feature food. Potluck, anyone?

Food brings people together. It relaxes you. It makes you feel connected to the people you are sharing the meal with. It makes you more willing to share your own thoughts and feelings and more receptive to what they have to say and more.

I know you're busy. I know the evenings are filled with activities. I know you don't always get home at the same time and even if you did get home early enough to cook dinner, you're too tired to do it. I know you may not like to cook, and maybe your partner doesn't either. Maybe you're on your own most nights and adding making dinner to your list of things to do sounds impossible. Maybe you have finicky eaters in the house, children and adults alike. I know, I really do.

I also know that magic happens around the table.

Get creative. If you don't like to cook, pick up take-out, then sit together and eat it as if you had made it yourselves. Get a frozen meal from the supermarket and bake it in the oven. Simple grilled cheese can be very comforting after a long day; add a bagged salad from the store, and you have a meal. Put everything on a real plate and set the table as if eating together is important—because it is.

If you get home too late to start cooking, dust off the slow cooker and prep the food in the morning, or even on your day off, and put it all in the fridge, pre-measured and chopped, then start it in the morning before you go to work. There is nothing like coming in the door tired and hungry and smelling a homemade meal ready to eat.

Have a basket or tray or just a spot in another room where everyone puts their phones, including guests, for the duration of the meal. This is not only a Blackout habit, but a good habit for life. Don't think about snapping photos of food and posting about how good it is. Simply enjoy the flavors and relax in good company.

As you go through the Blackout, you'll realize it isn't just for the children. Most adults experience improvement in their relationships, including those with people who aren't blacking out.

My friend Amy frequently hosts dinners with friends, and she has a no-phone policy at the table, no exceptions. All phones are placed in a basket and put in the next room. Near enough to hear if there were a true emergency, but not close enough to be distracted by every notification. One of her regular guests has a large Instagram following and works in a field where marketing and the arts intersect. She uses her posts to promote herself and her business, so they have reached a compromise. Before everyone sits down, her friend snaps a photo of the place settings and the untouched food. Then she puts her phone away, sometimes after a group shot with the other guests, and the true meal begins.

Some people didn't like her policy when she first began, but after a few awkward minutes, her guests forgot to be offended. Now, many of her friends leave their phones in their cars altogether, knowing they won't need them inside. And this hasn't hurt her popularity. At least once a week, she has a house full of hungry friends, talking and laughing together.

Amy enjoys hosting and likes to cook. Obviously, that is not everyone. Luckily, there are options.

If budgeting and planning stress you out, there are meal planning services that create a list for you based on your dietary preferences and your local stores' sales. They are very reasonably priced. You can also find entire meal prep shops where you can either create meals yourself on site or pick up prepared dishes and simply bake at home. Visiting a meal prep shop and putting together a few dinners is an excellent activity to do with an older child who enjoys working in the kitchen.

If you like to cook but don't have the time or inclination to shop and plan, look into meal delivery kits like Blue Apron, Hello Fresh, and Sun Basket. They send everything you need for a meal (or two or three) in a box that arrives at your home. Most meals are moderately priced and can be really fun to prepare. Cooking together is an excellent way to bond with your children and with your spouse. Many delivery companies offer specialty food plans if you follow a specific diet. And no matter how old they are, kids love packages. When the box arrives, they will rush towards it and eagerly read the instructions. It's a great way to try new and unusual food for your family.

I don't expect you to do this every night, but twice a week is an excellent and realistic goal. You'd be surprised how many people don't sit down with the family to eat. Think about it. When was the last time you sat down with your entire family and shared a meal? All the kids, your partner, sitting at one table and actually talking to each other. And, no, pizza in front of the television doesn't count.

While you're doing the Blackout, having activities can help to get through the tough spots and create opportunities to spend time with each other. After the halfway point, it will feel more natural, but prior to that, having a game plan can help.

Start with one meal. Look at the calendar. Find a day that no one has practice or rehearsals or tutoring after six o'clock. Choose how you're going to eat—take-out, a meal from scratch, some sort of kit or ready-made food. Write it on the calendar. (Side note: A paper calendar on the wall in a prominent location can be helpful. The entire family can see it, and a quick glance to check the schedule won't lead you down the rabbit-hole of notifications and text messages like checking the calendar on your phone can do.)

Once your meal is scheduled, tell the family. "We're having dinner together Thursday night at 6:30. Meet me at the table."

Most children like to be involved in this process. The first time might be a little tricky, but depending on your kids' ages and personal talents, you can give them a portion of the meal to be in charge of. My friend Amy of the no-phones-at-the-table rule, involves the entire family in the process. Her youngest child, at six, sets the table. She enjoys choosing the tablecloth and napkins and putting everything on the table just so. If you have a child with an artistic bent, this is likely a chore they will enjoy. It's also the most sought-after chore in Amy's house.

Her oldest child, at 13, will often make a dish herself from start to finish. When she was younger, she would help rinse and chop vegetables. Now, she can nearly make her own meal from scratch. Her 10-year-old son enjoys tasks that resemble building or putting things together. He likes to chop all the ingredients for a salad or plate the food according to the instructions, watching all the individual pieces come together to create the final product. If you have a child who enjoys playing with Legos or something similar, or even playing Minecraft, there's a good chance they will enjoy the building aspects of meal creation.

Meals at Amy's house are always lively. Everyone takes turns telling the best and worst parts of their day, something they call High/Low. It gives everyone a chance to talk and keeps them in the loop with each other's lives, not unlike the Rose/Bud/Thorn activity we do at home. When the meal is finished, they all carry the dishes into the kitchen and the cleanup is done together, often with music in the background.

So much is accomplished in this simple tradition. The family spends time together, builds trust, and bonds because they are having fun with one another. As an added bonus, the children learn real-life skills: responsibility (don't forget about your timer!), how to work on a team (she does the potatoes, he makes the salad), and even risk management (walk slowly with a full glass of water, carry the knives sharp side down, don't touch the burner if it's red.) Not to mention that everyone sleeps better when their tummies are full and their basic emotional needs are met—bedtime after family dinners is usually a snap.

Local Field Trips

Taking a field trip with your kid isn't feasible every day, but they are perfect for weekends and can be a wonderful way to spend time on summer break and other school holidays. Highlight or bookmark the pages with activities you want to try.

- Museums – Check out any museums near you. Sometimes the most unusual ones are the most interesting. Maybe there is one detailing the life of a local celebrity or politician. There might be a museum dedicated to classic cars or quilt making or rug weaving. Many have certain days you can get in free with a canned good or other small donation to a local charity.
- Historic tours – Tours are great for weekends and holidays. Check out historic homes, civic buildings, and battle sites. Some will have a fee, others will be free.
- Walking tours – Many towns (if not yours, maybe one nearby) offer walking tours of the city's sites. They last anywhere from one to three hours, keep you moving, and teach you a lot along the way. If you really want to take it to the next level, find out what your kids are studying in school and find a tour that coincides with their curriculum. If you can't find a tour you like, consider taking a few hours to walk through a town with historic markers. Make a point to go to each one and read it thoroughly, maybe even read a book about the people, places, or events it describes before you go.
- Food tours – These types of tours can be great for teenagers, especially if they are a little adventurous. You can find food tours of almost any type, and it can be a great way to bond with an older child. They can

be pricey, but doing it once during the Blackout, or even as the final night celebration, can be fun. If you can't find a suitable tour near you, consider doing your own progressive dinner. Go one place for an appetizer, another for a side salad, the third for a main course, and another for dessert. Have your teenager plan where to go and make any necessary reservations. This is also a fun way to celebrate a special occasion.

- Staycation – If you have kids with you for long periods of time, for example, if they are on a break from school or you homeschool or they are very young, consider acting like a tourist in your own town or a nearby town. Walk around downtown, see whatever sites are available (lakes, waterfalls, interesting architecture, etc.), and try a new restaurant.

Daily or Weekly Options

- Library – Get to know your library. Most libraries, including those in small towns, have a variety of activities for children of all ages. The options are endless. I've seen various story times, craft projects, Lego groups, mystery nights, crocheting classes, photography classes, the list goes on. And everything is FREE.
- Take a class – Signing up for a class at your local rec center, learning center, or other organization can be a way to bond with your child as well as fill those "Now what?" moments. These are especially good for older children. Take a class in cooking, foreign language, dance, music, creative writing, painting, whatever suits your fancy. These are also a great way to bond with your spouse if you can sneak away for an evening.

- Shop Class – Most big box hardware stores like Home Depot and Lowes offer classes on the weekends for various projects like putting up backsplashes, installing doorknobs, simple woodworking projects, etc. These are useful, fun, and often appeal to kids who like doing things with their hands or who have an eye for dimensions.
- Virtual Design – By virtual, I mean imaginary, not computerized. Sketch out a house floor plan on graph paper or printer paper or whatever you have handy. Better yet, get your child to do it. Then design the house. Younger kids can make certain rooms tree house rooms and fairy rooms, older kids might get more sophisticated with their design. This is a common activity on a popular online game, and you'd be surprised how many kids enjoy it. You can go to local furniture stores and choose pieces that would go in your imaginary house. Let them look in old magazines and cut out pictures of rooms and homes they like. You could follow this up with a walk through a neighborhood with a specific form of architecture, maybe historic, or super modern, or specifically Victorian or Craftsman or mid-century. They could make a collage out of magazine pictures and their own photos, all on the theme of their house.
- Games – Games, games, and more games. It doesn't have to be complicated like a drawn out round of Monopoly or Settlers of Catan. It can be a simple card game. Go Fish is great for young children, and you'd be surprised how quickly they can learn in-depth card games. Try Rummy, Double or Triple Solitaire, Speed, Slap Jack, Phase Ten, Sequence, Uno, Skip-Bo, etc. Just about any board game will do. Go to the local second-hand store and see what they have. Goodwill and Salvation Army generally have a decent selection. Taboo, Blokus, Cranium, and Trivial Pursuit are all fun and great for older kids who like a

143

mental challenge. Pictionary, Picture/Picture, and Pictureka are good for artistic kids. Try Scattergories for the vocabulary maven.

I know it can be daunting to suddenly have a child with you who doesn't know how to have fun without a screen. If you have one or more children with you all day, it gets especially hairy. There are only so many pictures you can color and crafts you can make.

This is when I recommend getting outside. Children need to learn to manage risk on their own, and they do that through playing with adult *supervision*, but not adult *intervention*. Go to your local park. Let them play on the playground as long as you can. If they are old enough to run around without you, take a book or magazine to peruse.

If you have a yard, utilize it. Most kids need significantly more time outside than they are getting. If it's hot, turn on the sprinkler and get them in a bathing suit. If it's snowing, build a snowman or make snow angels.

Many parks or libraries are built near water, generally a small river or stream. Get your child a pair of rain boots (I recommend the local Goodwill, Salvation Army, or thrift store for cheap finds), a bucket, and a small shovel. Bring a camp chair for yourself. Let them go to town playing in the mud with rocks and water. It looks senseless, but they are learning and adapting to their environment. They are managing risk. They are building confidence. **Let them play.**

If the weather is cold, try going to the bowling alley. Some have memberships that are inexpensive and some even offer free games to kids during summer break if it's before a certain time of day. Skating rinks are also an excellent option. It's bilateral movement, which helps to restore a dysregulated nervous system, and it gets the blood flowing and can raise endorphins.

Taking a walk is always a good idea—it's more bilateral movement. If the weather isn't conducive to an outdoor walk, try a nearby mall or any store big enough to allow for a few laps: Wal-Mart, Target, Home Depot, Costco, Sam's, Bass Pro, etc.

Of course, you can always read books, you to them, them to you, and everyone on their own. You can listen to audio books or story dramatizations as a sole activity or while you fold laundry or do other chores together. You can do puzzles together.

Teach them to do chores. Children can be helpful at surprisingly young ages. They can fold clothes, put away dishes, sweep, mop (though it might be best to start with only a wet cloth), dust, and organize. Chores teach them practical skills and give a sense of *real* self-confidence. They can look at the stack of folded towels with pride, knowing they did that on their own. They can watch something go from dirty to clean or from chaos to order and see the change before their eyes. That's instant gratification with positive reinforcement.

1. What are you doing with your free time? Is it torture to think of something to do or does it come easily? Write down and commit to two activities you will do with your children this week.
2. Have you been eating together more? How is dinner going? How often do you do it?
3. Are you cooking together at all? Choosing what to order together? Setting the table together? If your kids are not involved in meal preparation or serving, go ahead and plan one night this week to make (or order) and eat dinner together.
4. How are your children dealing with new activities without screens?
5. Hang a calendar in an easy-to-find location. My favorite kind has columns for different family members to keep everyone organized. There's a link in Resources at the end of the book. Make sure it's hung at a level where kids can see it.

Interview with Celia

as told to Elizabeth Adams

Celia is a Nashville-based author and mother. Her family did the Blackout last summer for 30 days. With no school for distraction, mom working from home, and five kids in the house, it wasn't easy.

"It was awful," says Celia.

Summer is when all the emotional turmoil in her kids' lives comes to a head anyway, due to the fact that everyone is thrown together for long periods of time. Add in the Blackout and the usual drama of five kids between the ages of 12 and 16, and it gets interesting.

"When everyone's home, things will get tumultuous."

They originally started the Blackout for her son, Matthew. He couldn't access his emotions properly and he was having difficulty expressing himself and his feelings. Communication was stalled. So they went to see Stacy for help, and she recommended the Blackout.

The whole family did it together, though both parents made modifications for work. Celia works from home, but she has a separate office so she's able to be on the computer away from the kids.

Celia said it was rough in the beginning. "They thought they were going to die. You would have thought we'd said no food or water for 30 days."

Celia and her husband hit on a solution. "We did cheat a little and bribe them. When they went back to school in the fall, we were going to get them new phones." So Celia told the kids that in order to prove they could be responsible with technology going forward, the family would do this Blackout period so they would know they could live without it.

The first week was the worst. The hardest part? "Honestly, just breaking the addiction to the phone, or the TV, or whatever else."

They had to develop an entire life away from technology, which they hadn't done since they were small children. They had to learn to play games, communicate with their friends, and entertain themselves without screens of any kind.

To smooth the transition, they took the kids shopping for unplugged activities: board games, puzzles, and books.

"We worked a 2000-piece family puzzle that month. Taking that shopping trip early on and letting them pick how they wanted to spend the next 30 days really helped them take ownership of it," says Celia.

The second week things got better.

"I thought they'd be at each other's throats because there were no distractions, but fighting went down," says Celia. "They actually started to communicate with each other and get along. Sibling relationships took the place of their dependency on electronics. The longer we did it, the better it got."

The two youngest boys often fought for the position of baby in the family and were in constant conflict. One day, Celia thought she heard the boys fighting and rushed upstairs.

"They had set up their own little basketball court in their room and were playing and laughing. We were all just kind of shocked. That relationship especially got better."

Relationships across the board were improving.

"We spent a lot more time together—quality time together for the first time in a long time," says Celia. "Because I was really strict with my business hours, it allowed me to really set aside time with my kids every day."

Nearly a year later, their technology use is close to where they were before the Blackout with some notable differences.

"They interact with each other more. They're outside a lot more, nearly every day," says Celia. "That really surprised me. They're spending more time with each other."

The family hasn't decided if they will take a technology break this summer, but they are considering how to fit it in.

"I will say that after the Blackout was over with, they were actually glad we did it. They enjoyed it and they were so shocked that they liked it."

7

After the Blackout

It never ceases to amaze me how a family can be so resistant to the mere thought of the Blackout in the beginning, and by the end of the 30 days be so grateful for the positive impact it has made in their lives. After leading hundreds of families through the Blackout, it is clear the benefits far outweigh the sacrifice.

After the Blackout concludes, most parents ask what they need to do moving forward to build upon the success the family realized during the Blackout. Parents intuitively know that if they go back to allowing as much screen time as they used to, then all of the progress the family has made over the preceding 30 days will start to fall away.

Moving forward, I tell families to consider entertainment-based screen time as the dessert of their lives instead of the main course. Parents need to ensure that the family's top priority is developing and maintaining meaningful connections among all family members.

Just as humans cannot live a healthy lifestyle by eating candy and cookies as their primary food source, children cannot thrive if electronic screens are the primary basis of their social connection and play time. Finding the appropriate place for entertainment-based screen time as a treat in your life instead of your primary sustenance is vital. It looks different for each family, but the important thing to remember is that the parents are in control of the family's screens; screens are not in control of the family.

Regardless of your career, community, or culture, you have the power to be in control of balancing your family's technological activities. Ideally, the parents will set up boundaries where screens will add value to their children's lives in a positive way. Alternatively, you could continue living like a robot with the screens being in control of your family. You have the power and freedom to decide.

I personally do not like feeling like a robot, and the majority of my clients feel the same way. But deciding to take control of your family's screens is a lifestyle change, much like stopping smoking or altering your eating habits. In the beginning it feels like punishment, but as time goes on, the freedom feels exhilarating.

Life is all about freedom to me. And boundaries around screen time bring freedom. The freedom to be present with your children, the freedom to take better care of yourself, and the freedom to put your values and priorities in the order that will make you feel good about how you spend your days. Aren't you tired of missing precious moments with your family because you are too busy checking Facebook or Instagram? You have the power and ability to make a change.

Now that you have made a conscious decision to build upon the success your family realized during the Blackout and exercise power over your screens, what happens next?

One option is to cortisol test your child and compare the pre- and post-Blackout test results. It is important that your child's cortisol levels are in a normal range for health, both physically and emotionally. You can look into at-home testing kits, such as those through www.livewelltesting.com, or consult your healthcare provider. This can give you an idea of where your child's stress levels were before and after the Blackout and help you decide what to do going forward.

Believe it or not, about half of my clients choose to do the Blackout again! Many parents see such benefits from the Blackout to their children's lives—behavior, level of happiness and contentment, willingness to participate in family activities, and ability to connect—that they want to ensure these new behaviors are ingrained and reinforced with another Blackout. And they typically come up with the idea of repeating it on their own.

There are some instances where I recommend doing a second Blackout. For some children, usually the ones with a more severe dependency on entertainment-based screen time, it literally feels like the kids have been holding their breath for 30 days and marking off the days in anticipation of when they will be getting their screens back.

This typically negates the purpose of the whole thing. I have found many children replay TV shows and video games in their minds in order to get the same hit they were used to, because they simply have not learned to live without their screens. They do not know how to manage their feelings, ask for their needs to be met, or even just sit quietly. Neither do their parents, so the Blackout in many ways is an introduction to the simple things in life.

Following the Blackout, one argument I get a lot is, "How is my child going to interact with his friends since they're used to playing video games together?!"

Here is what I have found. When a child is grounded in connection in family life, many of these things become a non-issue. Even though there may not be as many children outside playing and meeting at parks, libraries, and nature centers as there used to be—they *are* out there. There are other parents out there just like you who want to connect in real and meaningful ways. It just takes more effort these days to find them. And in an ironic twist, technology can help you do just that. There are numerous parent groups online organizing play dates and other events. Find them. Many kid-centered places will have a calendar of events. There are ways. **You can make this work.**

Playing video games is not always a bad thing as long as it is done in moderation. Spending 30 minutes at an arcade or playing video games (preferably not the killing or shooting kind) with friends at home is fine. But be aware of the consequences of this action.

I have found that the fast-paced, high-intensity video games can dysregulate children's nervous systems. The next thing you know, they don't want to take ballet class anymore, or go to the park, or practice piano or help cook in the kitchen, because all their nervous system wants to do is reprocess a video game they were not developmentally ready to experience in the first place.

And is this really worth it? I mean, think about it. The truth is, they are sitting on their behinds twirling their thumbs while staring at a screen. Is that really worth losing precious childhood hours and days over? Is it worth exchanging wonder and discovery for a few hours of mindless entertainment?

I find the families who choose to do the Blackout twice, especially if they really need it, are the most convinced that their former way of life can no longer continue. The second Blackout gives more time for life to slow down and more opportunities for intentionality around planning connection-based activities.

These are the families who truly begin to experience delighting in each other. They enjoy each other's company more. They help each other. They have the time to resolve conflict in meaningful ways. They sit and reflect and think about what is truly important to them, where they want to go as a family, as a team. They are thinking more clearly about what they really want in life.

That is the gift of rest.

The gift of rest is recalibration. It's a sense of calm, a stillness that helps us slow down. It is a meditation of sorts, an opportunity to listen thoughtfully and to find a new rhythm with life and the relationships we hold dear.

It is a loving intervention to bring more joy to your day, more love to your relationships, and more heart-to-heart conversations. It is a time of peace, a time of reflection.

You are worth it. Your family is worth it.

And isn't it about time?

Now that you have completed your Blackout(s), what comes next? Don't go back to unlimited, unfettered access to screens. Just like eating junk food all day will cause you to regain all the weight you lost on your diet, using screens like you used to will put you right back where you started.

The key is using screens within limits, and every family situation is different.

After the Blackout, I recommend families implement a time blocking system that clearly delineates who is doing what and when they are doing it. This system provides everyone in the family with a clear understanding of when parents are working, when family time happens, and when a family dinner can be expected. It also outlines when leisure screen time occurs as well as when the family will do bonding activities together that do not involve screens.

Some of my favorite non-electronic activities to do as a family include going on nature walks, cooking in the kitchen, reading books, doing arts and crafts, going swimming, and playing board games. I suggest you incorporate a few of these activities into your weekly routine.

This next part is an important step—please don't skip it.

I also strongly urge parents to download Net Nanny or other parental watch service on every screen you own—every phone, iPad, tablet and TV in the house, even the parents'. The site www.protectyoungeyes.com can connect you to these and other helpful resources. These services will allow you to set an age limit of appropriateness on your family's devices. My suggestion is to set it a level younger than the child's current age. This service will filter out all the violence, pornography, and other unnecessary drama that your child does not need to be exposed to. Children are exposed to enough secondary information via marketing and other communications in their day-to-day lives. We don't need to give them unlimited access to inappropriate material on our screens.

Another tool I recommend for your phones and tablets is the Screen Time app (screentimelabs.com). It is particularly helpful for adults and older children. You simply set an amount of time per day that you want to allow for screen time, and then the app will pause the device once the limit is met. This app also sends an email to the caregiver each time your child installs an app, and it sends a daily diary of everything your child did on the device that day.

Many phones come with something like this built in. Some home internet providers also offer similar services, where you can limit the Wi-Fi in your house regardless of what device is connected to it. You can set your home or work router to filter out adult content for free using clean DNS servers (see opendns.com and cleanbrowsing.org). This can be useful if you frequently have visitors.

I like the Screen Time app because it helps set healthy boundaries and requires an adolescent child (or adult for that matter) to use their time wisely. Say goodbye to the days of mindless scrolling, losing hours of your time doing who-knows-what. It's time to use screens for what they were designed for—convenience, information, efficiency, fun (in moderation), and reaching those who are important to us.

Don't go back to this!

Another recommendation I have for younger children (those in the play years under the age of 10), is the Screen Time Marble System mentioned in Chapter 6.

You give each child a jar containing seven marbles. Each marble equals 30-45 minutes per day of screen time. The child has the opportunity to spend their screen time as they wish—a little bit each day or a few at a time, like for a weekend movie night. They get to choose, but that is all the screen time they get until the following week. Parents also have their own stash of marbles and have the option of adding a marble to their child's jar to reward good behavior, or they can take a marble away for misbehaving. If that sounds like a lot of work, know that you don't have to do it forever. Some families like the regulation it provides and will use it long-term. Others use it until a new normal is established, then they gradually stop using the marbles and simply rely on their new habits.

One of my favorite traditions in our family is something I recommend to all families after they complete the Blackout—a movie night at home. Yes, it's just like it sounds. Pop some popcorn and snuggle up on the couch to watch a family movie together. This is a great way to use your screen time in a positive way. There are more children's movies made now than ever before—it shouldn't be difficult to find something appropriate.

Here is something important to keep in mind. If the TV is constantly on in the background every day, family movie nights don't seem as special. Get used to your TV and phones being off (or silenced) on a regular basis. To that end, allocate your time by planning ahead and outlining when it's time to work, when it's time to sleep, when it's time to play, and so forth.

This will create an environment where you have less split attention. Split attention is when you are paying attention to your phone and trying to have a conversation with your child at the same time. Most children will simply perceive this as you not listening to them. I know this because I've been guilty of it, too.

The 30 Day Blackout takes intentionality, encouragement, and the adoption of a new culture in your family. Thankfully, there is a path for you to follow. View this journey as an adventure, and before long, you and your family will be that much further up the mountain.

Celebrate!

One of the most rewarding elements of finishing something difficult—climbing a mountain, running a marathon, passing a class—is the celebration when you finally cross the finish line. You get to throw your hands in the air and feel the glory of having finished something hard and worthwhile.

At the conclusion of your Blackout, it's time to celebrate the successes and accomplishments your family has realized. Even if you are not yet seeing all of the results you were hoping for, your family has likely made great strides. The fact that you had a singular focus on improving your family's lifestyle for the previous 30 days is a significant accomplishment, one that should be celebrated and appreciated. Your family's journey is something each of you should take great pride in.

Go out for a nice dinner all together, take the kids to see a play or musical, maybe go on a day trip somewhere you've been wanting to go. Let your children see that they accomplished something great and that it is being rewarded.

After your family takes a step back and rejoices in making it this far in the journey, I think you will find that many more celebrations will occur on a regular basis. For many of my clients, the simple events in daily life become joyous. A family dinner with uninterrupted conversation becomes something to look forward to. A walk around the block or bike ride to visit the neighbors becomes an enjoyable little adventure. A trip to the park is a relaxing getaway. Truly enjoying one another's company is rewarding and fulfilling. Seeing, hearing, and celebrating another person that you hold dear is one of life's true pleasures. Holding their hand, looking into their eyes, and seeing life from their point of view is what life and relationship is all about. And now that your family is on the other side of 30 Day Blackout, you can enjoy your new lifestyle.

After the Blackout, most parents I work with celebrate their child's ability to be more compliant in day-to-day interactions, with less push back and more go-with-the-flow. Many parents report their child can focus for longer periods of time, clean their room by themselves (this is a big one), and are able to stay better organized. Many parents also claim fewer tantrums and meltdowns and comment that their children can quietly read in contentment. Their moods are more easily regulated, and some parents report children having better manners. I have even seen medications lessened or eliminated altogether (under a doctor's supervision, of course), which is something to celebrate. Parents are celebrating that their child is sleeping more soundly, having fewer nightmares, and experiencing a new level of empathy for others, especially siblings. Many families celebrate that they are less stressed, more relaxed, and happier.

If someone told you there was a way to feel happier, more relaxed, and to have less stress in your life, would you pay attention? What if it cost you nothing and only required a month of intense effort for a lifetime of residual benefits? Wouldn't you be willing to make that effort? To make that sacrifice for the greater gain?

That's what the Blackout is. An intense effort for 30 days, and an enormous gain in peace, calm, joy, empathy, kindness, compassion, relaxation, and contentment. Pleasure in daily life again. Joy in the middle of a rainy Tuesday afternoon. Calm when you would normally be stressed, peace when you would usually be anxious.

I even have families return to the old-fashioned art of letter writing to family and friends. There's something about slowing down and resetting the body's clock to a more natural state that encourages a family's willingness to enjoy the simple things in life. Screens are no longer being used as a stimulant, therefore the child's nervous system is being optimized as it was designed to be—utilizing the ventral parasympathetic branch for a sense of feeling "all is well" in the world.

That is something to celebrate.

All these celebrations remind us that screens do not have to rule our lives. They prove that we can leave our phones in a drawer at night to make a clear statement that our family time is a priority. They show that being hijacked by a phone is no longer the life we choose to live. We can set boundaries that create freedom for ourselves and our children, like having screen-free rooms in our homes and designated times when we are available to use a screen.

As parents, we realize our children watch and emulate what we model for them. No more scrolling through our phones while lying in bed or talking to our children while looking at social media or sitting in a restaurant texting or playing a video game. It's time to hang up and hang out with your kids in one-on-one, respectful interaction. Demonstrate to them that these little computers in our pockets do not merit the privilege of ruling our lives or our children's lives.

Choosing pro-social, educational "slow screen time" content adds value to our children's lives and social experiences. This looks different for each family, but being mindful and intentional about what we want our children and families exposed to takes honest dialogue, healthy boundary setting, and a good kitchen timer. Scheduling screen time around real life, rather than real life around screens, is key. And I've never seen a family regret it.

The Power of Rest

I think many people would agree that most of us have forgotten how to rest. The hustle and bustle of modern life, despite our best intentions, has forced so many of us into a web of busyness where we get stuck more often than we care to admit.

I remember a dear father in my office, a high-powered CEO and wealthy man with four children, who thought he was in my office because he couldn't fix his marriage. His children were highly disrespectful, and his work had taken over his life. He was a prisoner of the "golden handcuffs," as he called them. It was a train he desperately wanted to jump off, but the lifestyle he had created, along with a wife who loved to spend money, held him hostage. Or so he thought.

I asked him, "What is your favorite childhood memory where you felt all was well and peaceful in your world?"

After a few moments of contemplation, this big, burly man remembered when he would lie down beneath the family oak tree as a child, and he would look up and watch the clouds roll by for hours. "Not a care in the world," he reminisced, as tears rolled down his face.

His life was nothing but cares now. His extreme will to succeed stemmed back to his early years when he played the role of "hero" in his family. His father told him that he would be proud of him when he made it "to the top." Those words drove him his entire life, even though he wasn't aware of it. His resume, accomplishments, and accolades were truly impressive, not to mention the lifestyle, home, private schooling, and luxury vacations he could afford. And yet, tears rolled down this man's face just at the thought of having a single day to lie on his back and watch the clouds roll slowly by like when he was a child.

It was that day, along with many other days like it throughout my career, that convinced me it really is the little things that matter in life. And one of those little things that is so important, and yet we somehow have forgotten, is stepping back and simply resting.

Rest from striving, rest from comparing, rest from resentment, rest from entertainment, rest from consumerism, and yes, rest from screens. Time to simply be still and unplug.

As I mentioned earlier, years ago in my early 20s, I was sitting on the front porch of a cabin with no electricity, newly married and in the midst of a life-changing adventure. I had no children yet and all the time in the world. My husband and I were what I call "commuter pioneers," meaning we were living for a time in this cabin to experience life unplugged. We both had jobs working in the city, and on this particular morning, my husband was about to leave for work.

As I sat on the front porch of this rustic 1850s cabin, all I did was notice things around me.

I noticed the wind swaying the trees. I noticed the clear blue sky. I noticed the sheltered, protected feeling I had sitting on the front porch of a cabin that had been there for 150 years. The aged wood of the porch, the creaking of the rocking chair, the songs of birds in the trees all came together with the green grass and rich brown dirt to ground me.

I really have no idea what I was thinking about, but I do remember I felt I had been sitting there for a long time. It seemed like an eternity.

I looked down at my watch and it was 9:15 in the morning. Only 15 minutes had passed. I was amazed at how peaceful and relaxed I felt—given my background and childhood, 15 minutes of peace was like handing me gold bars on a platter. I needed little else in my life at that moment.

I share this with you because sometimes all we need is 15 minutes of uninterrupted "be" time. Fifteen minutes with no agenda, no screens, no to-do list, to just let our hearts and minds find rest. To just be.

It is in these peaceful moments where our minds and bodies are recalibrated and restored for the next step in our journey.

No one knows if you or I will live to be 100 years old, or even make it through tomorrow. But I do know this: If we are honest with ourselves, we all would admit that we want to experience more *real* life and less *virtual* life; more connection and less longing; more friendship and less loneliness; more true acceptance and less false approbation. Most of us crave solid, meaningful time with our families and friends. And that, in essence, is why I started the Blackout. Not to torture people, but to give them an intentional way to pause, to recalibrate, to just be. And most importantly, to connect.

The truth is, in order to optimize the cognitive, emotional, social, and moral development of our children, we must allow them an opportunity to rest. The Blackout allows for better, more meaningful relationships. It allows for increased emotional closeness because the environment in which they live is now quiet enough to talk to each other about things that matter. It allows for wider interests and exploration because children actually have an opportunity and freedom to try interesting things without their brains being hijacked.

Connection is the lifeblood of our existence. This book has been about how technology interrupts that connection, but it's possible to interrupt it in other ways. Some people will avoid connection out of fear. Others avoid it out of anger or some other emotion.

Screens are the primary choice of most of us today, deliberately or otherwise, for avoiding people and conversations we'd rather not have. But there are other ways of alienating ourselves and limiting connection to others. Be aware of another activity you may need to Blackout. Do you ignore your kids to go exercise for hours a day? Do you have a hobby that takes a large portion of your time at the expense of your family? Are you spending too much time at your job?

Have you ever gotten in a car with someone and they immediately turned the music up as loud as possible and ignored you when you tried to speak with them? They successfully avoided connection without using a screen.

I have a friend whose mother spent two years of her childhood locked in her room reading. She would come out to prepare meals, then go right back to her room. She was clearly depressed after her recent divorce, but her children were essentially raising themselves while she was licking her wounds.

I know a man who enjoyed building model airplanes. He set up a room in his basement and worked on them every spare moment he had. It was an enjoyable activity for him, but he never involved his wife or his grandchildren, and when the family came over and things got too noisy for him, he retreated to his plane room where everyone knew they were not welcome. He was missing out on his family, and he didn't require a screen to do it.

Screens cause all kinds of damage, from the nervous system to brain development to the loss of connection in families. Other activities like exercise and model building may not disrupt a person's nervous system or brain development, and may even have other physical benefits, but they can still get in the way of connecting with loved ones.

Take a good look and be honest with yourself. If you need to make adjustments, have the courage to do so. Connecting with your kids is worth it.

165

Take a Break

An element I suggest to many of my families post-Blackout is a weekly technology break. Just like a day of physical rest is known to help regulate mood and appetite and re-energize our bodies, a technology sabbath of sorts clears waste from our brain and helps us reset.

A technology break is one day each week that allows us to utilize technology's best feature—the off switch—to let our brains rest. By coming back into regulation—scientifically speaking, engaging the ventral branch of the parasympathetic nervous system on a regular basis by disengaging from a heightened state—we are now able to use technology for its original intent, which is to add value to life rather than detract from it.

The break allows the brain and nervous system an opportunity to rest, heal and repair. A time to find connection, a simple 24-hour period of rest—for example Saturday night to Sunday night—for quiet reflection to read books, take naps, engage in outdoor activities, or simply use a pen and paper for a change.

It won't kill you. I promise.

Another element I recommend to many of my families post-Blackout is one week per year with very little electronic activity. How about a staycation filled with fun screen-free activities in your own town? Or a week at the beach where cooking together and making sandcastles and visiting the dolphins takes the place of scrolling through your social media feeds or watching TV? Perhaps you can even resist the temptation to post photos of your vacation to social media every day. (I know it's hard, but you CAN refrain.) Or a few days camping or visiting a lake where the focus in on rest, rejuvenation, and playful connection rather than constant entertainment.

I have found that enhancing family life with these practices will repair the exhausted brain, calm an overwhelmed nervous system, and result in dramatic improvement in children's health and behavior. Children also typically make better grades, have more engaged social interaction, show improved compliance, and are more focused and organized.

Spread the Word

I'm not the only one who wants to spread the word about this issue. I know a precocious little 7-year-old girl who became what I call a 30 Day Blackout ambassador. Although she was not my primary client, she was definitely a thankful participant in her family's two Blackouts.

She became so convinced that the Blackout had helped not only her, but also her entire family, that she had to tell everyone. While at a neighbor's house one day, she assessed and determined that her neighbors needed a "talking to," as she put it.

This little girl took it upon herself to sit down the entire neighbor's family to explain to them that she was not trying to hurt their feelings, but that it was high time they learned about the 30 Day Blackout.

She told them of how her family turned off all the screens for 30 days. She talked about how hard it was at first, but then how so many wonderful things followed. She went on to tell the neighbors how important it is for a family to put down the screens and connect again.

I was so honored and impressed by this little child's bravery and boldness, that it solidified in my mind the necessity of getting the word out about the 30 Day Blackout so more families in need would be aware of its profound impact.

And so I ask you, will you be bold like this little 7-year-old and be a 30 Day Blackout ambassador? Will you tell your friends and neighbors about your Blackout experience and what it did for you and your family?

I truly believe that the advancement of technology has moved faster than our ability to keep it in its proper perspective. If we can commit to the responsible use of technology in our lives, we can make our world a better place.

We can choose calm over noise. We can choose sunlight over screen time. We can choose time to ourselves and with each other over being torn in a dozen different directions. It's worth it. It's necessary.

1. What is your plan for screens going forward? Marble system? Time-blocking chart?
2. Do you plan to do a second Blackout or a Grayout?
3. Have you and your family begun to reclaim everyday joy? What does that look like?
4. Is your Blackout Box full? Read through what you put in there to remind yourself of all you've accomplished.
5. Have you celebrated or made a plan to? You should! It's a big achievement!
6. How can you incorporate calming activities into your life?
7. Can you commit to spending three minutes every day noticing your surroundings and grounding yourself?
8. What activities can you do with your child to help him/her be more mindful? Deep breathing? Meditation? Yoga? Quiet time?

Mindfulness Exercise

We talked about mindfulness earlier in the book. Mindfulness is being present in the here and now, experiencing life in real time, not allowing distractions to split your focus in six directions at once.

To help ground you, and teach your kids to ground themselves, here is an exercise I want you to try. Please follow the instructions as stated. You might be surprised by what comes up. Begin with putting your phone on silent and in another room. Turn off any and all electronic devices in the room with you.

Take a deep breath, way down into your belly. In through your nose and out through your mouth. It's okay if you're noisy.

Take another.

Take one more.

Now look around you. What do you see?

Take another deep breath.

What do you smell?

Take another breath.

What do you hear?

Take another breath.

Close your eyes for a few minutes and focus on nothing but the sounds and smells around you. If other senses like touch and taste intrude, that's okay. Just continue to return your attention to what you hear and smell.

Keep breathing steadily.

Open your eyes.

Do you feel any different? What did you notice?

Reflect for a minute on that.

Do this exercise three or four times a week. It only takes a few minutes, and it grounds you in your environment. Once you've gotten the hang of it, you can try recalling a pleasant memory first, then with closed eyes, reach out to the environment in your memory in the same way. Wherever your mind takes you, do the same exercise.

Breathe.

Notice the sounds in your memory.

Another deep breath.

Notice the smells in your memory.

Another breath.

What do you see in your memory?

Keep breathing.

Rest here in this place. Don't rush.

When you're ready to leave the memory, open your eyes and take another breath. In through your nose, out through your mouth.

Notice the space around you.

Breathe.

Notice the sounds and smells around you.

Breathe.

This technique is called grounding and is used to center a person's focus onto the here and now. It is beneficial to everyone, children and adults alike. You may want to try guiding your child through a grounding exercise. Do it a few times a week and see if you or your child feel any more peaceful or less anxious.

"SOME TELEVISION PROGRAMS ARE LOUD AND
SCARY WITH PEOPLE SHOOTING OTHER PEOPLE. YOU
KNOW, YOU CAN DO SOMETHING ABOUT THAT. WHEN YOU
SEE SCARY THINGS ON TELEVISION, YOU CAN TURN IT OFF."
— FRED ROGERS

Resources

Family & Therapeutic Tools

You can download a copy of the Blackout Agreement at www.stacyjagger.com or make your own as outlined in Chapter 5.

Magic Mats: Communication-facilitating mats, available at www.stacyjagger.com

Kinesthetic toys: consider purchasing magnetic darts, a sand tray with rakes, or hand-sized squeeze/soft balls for a child experiencing a collapse response (shut down). Simple hand puppets are a great way for children to express their feelings.

Weighted blankets are soothing for some children who experience anxiety.

I recommend Theraplay's Activity Flip Book for finding ways to connect and play with your child. It's highly effective. Find it wherever you buy books.

Mom's Family Wall Calendar by Sandra Boynton – My favorite family calendar.

Parental Controls for Devices

Disney Circle Time App
Screen Time App
Net Nanny

All are available online or at the App Store and Google Play

For whole house monitoring try www.opendns.com and www.cleanbrowsing.org.

Support Organizations

Play Therapy International – www.playtherapy.org Sometimes you need back up.

Find a play therapist near you at www.a4pt.org

Synergetic Play Therapy Institute - www.synergeticplaytherapy.com For therapists, parents, and educators.

La Leche League – www.lllusa.org   When you have a new baby and you are nursing, you're in the parenting trenches. Get someone in there with you.

Attachment Parenting International www.attachmentparenting.org For information, tips, ideas, and group connections.

Music with Mommie – A Parent-Child bonding class found at StacyJagger.com

The Children's Success Foundation www.childrenssuccessfoundation.com

American Association for Marriage and Family Therapy – www.aamft.org

Emotional Focused Therapy, designed for couples but also used for families - www.iceeft.com

Recommended Slow-Action Shows

Remember to keep screens to a minimum post-Blackout.
When you do watch, try to limit it to slow-action shows
like the ones listed here. PBS Kids is a wonderful
resource and has many slow-action programs. Remember
to pay attention to your child. Sensitivity levels differ—
watch them and see how they react to various shows.

Mr. Rogers Neighborhood – available on Amazon Prime
Sesame Street – Try to find it on your local PBS station
Max and Ruby
Thomas the Train/Thomas and Friends
Curious George
Martha Speaks
Arthur
Wonder Pets
Sid the Science Kid
Backyardigans—This show occasionally has fast action
       episodes or scenes, but overall is slow and
       encourages imagination and creative play.
Shaun the Sheep – This one has no spoken or written
       language and is an excellent choice if English is
       not the child's first language.
Wallace and Grommet
I Love Lucy
Little House on the Prairie
The Walton's (This and other shows from the youth of
       older generations are often good choices and
       available at your local library or on a streaming
       service like Netflix or Amazon Prime. Think back
       to your childhood. What did you watch? Was it
       slow-action? Is it in line with your family's
       values? If the answers are yes, consider re-
       watching them with your kids now.)

Further Reading

The Last Child in the Woods by Richard Louv. This is my favorite on this list and unbelievably valuable. It is packed with good information about the impact of nature on a child's development.

Reset Your Child's Brain by Victoria L. Dunckley, MD. If you're looking for more information on this topic and an in-depth look at the brain, nervous system, and various diagnoses, check this out. For your inner scientist.

Glow Kids: How Screen Addiction is Hijacking Our Kids—and How to Break the Trance by Nicholas Kardaras. This is an in-depth look at the tech/screen problem and a fascinating read.

Siblings Without Rivalry by Adele Faber and Elaine Mazlish. If you have more than one child at home, this is a must.

The Five Love Languages by Gary Chapman is great for learning how to love your partner well. *The Five Love Languages of Children* by Gary Chapman and Ross Campbell, M.D. is along the same lines but adapted for the parent/child relationship. It is from a Christian perspective, but many of the principles are universal.

Peaceful Parent, Happy Kids by Dr. Laura Markham

The Connected Child: Bring Hope and Healing to Your Adoptive Family by Karyn B. Purvis, Ph.D., David R. Cross Ph.D., and Wendy Lyons Sunshine

Playful Parenting by Lawrence J. Cohen

I Love You Rituals by Becky A. Bailey, Ph.D.

Attachment-Focused Parenting: Effective Strategies to Care for Children by Daniel A. Hughes

Attached at the Heart: Eight Proved Principles for Raising Connected and Compassionate Children by Barbara Nicholson and Lysa Parker

The Attachment Connection: Parenting a Secure and Confident Child Using the Science of Attachment Theory by Ruth Newton and Allan Schore

The Whole-Brain Child: 12 Revolutionary Strategies to Nurture Your Child's Developing Mind by Daniel J. Siegel and Tina Payne Bryson

Transforming the Difficult Child: The Nurtured Heart Approach by Howard Glasser and Jennifer Easley

References

1. Bilton, N. (2014, September 10). Steve Jobs was a low-tech parent. *The New York Times*. Retrieved from https://www.nytimes.com/2014/09/11/fashion/steve-jobs-apple-was-a-low-tech-parent.html

2. Sulleyman, A. (2017, April 21). Bill Gates limits his children's use of technology. *The Independent*. Retrieved from https://www.independent.co.uk/life-style/gadgets-and-tech/news/bill-gates-children-no-mobile-phone-aged-14-microsoft-limit-technology-use-parenting-a7694526.html

3. Fleming, A. (2015, May 23). Screen time v play time: What tech leaders won't let their own kids do. *The Guardian*. Retrieved from https://www.theguardian.com/technology/2015/may/23/screen-time-v-play-time-what-tech-leaders-wont-let-their-own-kids-do

4. Ryan, J. (2019, July 23). School bans iPads and brings back paper text books. Retrieved from https://theheartysoul.com/school-banned-ipads-going-back-to-regular-textbooks/?utm_source=PPV

5. Does replacing textbooks with tablets impact student learning? (2019, April 23). Retrieved from https://www.studyinternational.com/news/does-replacing-textbooks-with-tablets-impact-student-learning/

6. American Academy of Pediatrics announces new recommendations for children's media use. (2016,

October 21). Retrieved from
https://www.aap.org/en-us/about-the-aap/aap-
press-room/Pages/American-Academy-of-
Pediatrics-Announces-New-Recommendations-
for-Childrens-Media-Use.aspx

7. Mark, A. E., M.sc, & Janssen, I., Ph.D. (2008, March
   28). Relationship between screen time and
   metabolic syndrome in adolescents. *Journal of
   Public Heath, 30*(2). Retrieved from
   https://academic.oup.com/jpubhealth/article/30/2/1
   53/15422218

8. Margalit, L., Ph.D. (2016, April 17). What screen time
   can really do to kids' brains. *Psychology Today.*
   Retrieved from
   https://www.psychologytoday.com/blog/behind-
   online-behavior/201604/what-screen-time-can-
   really-do-kids-brains

9. Media and young minds: Council on communications
   and media. (2016, November). *Pediatrics, 138*(5).
   Retrieved from
   https://pediatrics.aappublications.org/content/138/
   5/e20162591

10. Generation M2: Media in the lives of 8- to 18-year-
    olds. (2015, March 02). Retrieved from
    https://www.kff.org/other/event/generation-m2-
    media-in-the-lives-of/

11. Reduce screen time. (n.d.). Retrieved from
    https://www.nhlbi.nih.gov/health/educational/wec
    an/reduce-screen-time/index.htm

12. Dion, L. (2018). *Aggression in play therapy: A
    neurobiological approach for integrating
    intensity.* New York: W.W. Norton & Company.

13. O'Connor, K. J., Schaefer, C. E., & Braverman, L. D. (2016). *Handbook of play therapy*. Hoboken: Wiley.

   Adapted from Kevin O'Connor's *Color My Feelings* and Paris Goodyear Brown's *Color My Heart* intervention.

14. Booth, P. B., & Jernberg, A. M. (2010). *Theraplay: Helping parents and children build better relationships through attachment-based play.* San Francisco: Jossey-Bass.

15. Gehart, D. R. (2018). *Mastering competencies in family therapy: A practical approach to theories and clinical case documentation.* Australia: Cengage Learning.

Acknowledgements

It was a warm spring Sunday, and I had a touch of cabin fever. When my friend Elizabeth messaged me unexpectedly to see if I wanted to have lunch, I jumped at the chance. We hadn't seen each other for a while and between our collective seven children, schedules were hard to arrange.

It came up in our conversation that I had recently met Lauren Fulton, a Nashville-based public relations guru, and that she and her husband Brian had begun helping me get the word out about screen-time overuse and its effects on children.

The Fultons suggested I write a book to reach more people and I tried. I promise I really tried. But I am not a professional writer and between my family and a full-time practice, it felt like this book would never happen.

My friend Elizabeth just happens to be an author. That Sunday lunch turned out to be fate in action. We brainstormed ideas and talked details. I told her all about the Fultons and their tireless work on my behalf. We laughed and cried and dreamed together.

Then we planned this book.

I am so grateful for the help of my dedicated team. If it takes a village to raise a child, I'm convinced it takes a small town to publish a book.

I want to thank Brian Fulton and Fulton Health Strategies for their partnership and counsel throughout this process—for helping us bring this book to life and to all of you.

I have to express my deep sense of gratitude to my cowriter Elizabeth Adams who tirelessly poured her creativity and organizational prowess into this project. If we hadn't had lunch that Sunday, who knows if this book would have ever gotten off the ground.

My husband Ron Jagger is a selfless, dedicated husband and father who had faith in me and this project even when I was tired and tempted to give up. I couldn't ask for a better partner to have with me in the parenting trenches.

I want to thank my children for believing that their mama had something to say and that she needed to say it. Thank you from the bottom of my heart to "Uncle" Lynn Fuston who convinced me that writing this book was not only possible but necessary to help more children and families than could appear in my office.

Thank you to Martha and Bill Sears for lending their decades of wisdom and concern for children by supporting this endeavor.

Dr. Jim Coffield is a long-time friend and colleague whose love and support through the years have been instrumental in my career and personal life. He always knows just what to say when I need advice.

Chance Scoggins is a life coach extraordinaire, and he basically told me to run with this book idea back when I thought it was never going to happen. Look, Chance! We did it!

My assistant Brianna is a saint disguised as an organizing maven and I don't know what I would do without her.

Big thanks to Caitlin Daschner at Chromantic Studio for designing a gorgeous cover and to Cheyenne Cox for illustrations that got my point across in a simple image. Lori Lynn's editing skills are second to none. She made this book better and tighter than I thought it could be.

My colleagues Dr. Dianne Bradley, Stacy Phillips, Lynn Louise Wonders, Lisa Dion, Leanna Rae, Marnee Ferree, Barbie White, Laurie Proctor, Dr. James Wellborn, Dr. Ted Klontz, Dr. John Fite, and Dr. Teri

Murphy have been incredibly supportive of what I do and are fighting the good fight every day, face-to-face with families in their offices.

Brentwood United Methodist Church showed enormous faith in me when they offered me an office in their counseling service. Thank you.

Beth and Jim Hudgin changed my life when they agreed to let us live in their cabin all those years ago. Who knew it would lead me here? I'm more grateful than I can say.

Finally, to everyone who made it possible for this book to be written—by helping with kids, creating time for me and Elizabeth, or simply being a friend, thank you. To everyone who offered to read it and give feedback or write a review, thank you for your support and kindness in this endeavor.

From the bottom of my heart, thank you.

About the Authors

Stacy Jagger is a mother of four and a therapist to many. She is on a mission to restore wonder to childhood, connection to families, and intimacy to relationships.

She is the architect of the 30 Day Blackout, a break from technology designed to bring parents and children closer together and unleash the natural creativity in all of us. A musician at heart, she designed Music with Mommie, a parent-child bonding class that utilizes instruments and play to facilitate connection.

Stacy has spent the last several years of her career building Music City Family Therapy, her practice in Nashville, Tennessee. She lives on a small farm outside the city with her husband of twenty years, a pony named Mister Rogers, a few dozen chickens and a gaggle of ducks.

To find out more, go to StacyJagger.com.

Elizabeth Adams is a book-loving, tango-dancing former journalist who loves old houses and thinks birthdays should be celebrated with trips—as should most occasions. She can often be found by a sunny window with a cup of hot tea and a book in her hand.

She writes romantic comedy and comedic tragedy in both historic and modern settings, and she occasionally dusts off her sociology degree to write a little nonfiction.

You can find more information, short stories, and outtakes at <u>EAdamsWrites.com.</u>

Made in United States
Troutdale, OR
02/19/2024

17799840R00116